SYRIA

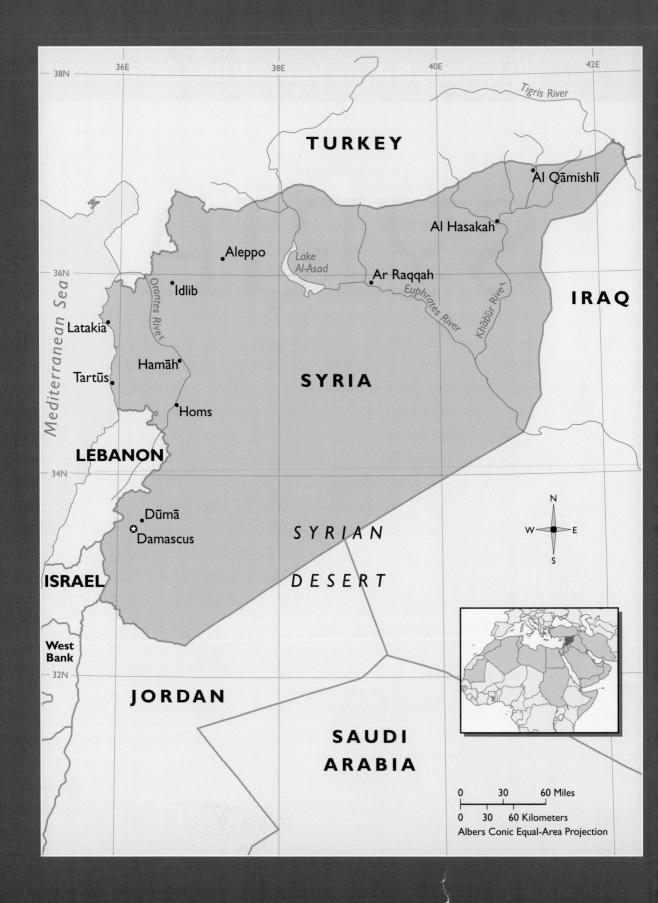

SYRIA

Anne Marie Sullivan

 MASON CREST
PHILADELPHIA

Mason Crest
450 Parkway Drive, Suite D
Broomall, PA 19008
www.masoncrest.com

Printed and bound in the United States of America.

CPSIA Compliance Information: Batch #MNMME2016.
For further information, contact Mason Crest at 1-866-MCP-Book.

3 5 7 9 8 6 4 2

Library of Congress Cataloging-in-Publication Data
        on file at the Library of Congress
            ISBN: 978-1-4222-3451-8 (hc)
            ISBN: 978-1-4222-8444-5 (ebook)

Major Nations of the Modern Middle East series ISBN: 978-1-4222-3438-9

TABLE OF CONTENTS

MAJOR NATIONS OF THE MODERN MIDDLE EAST

Afghanistan
Egypt
Iran
Iraq
Israel
Jordan
The Kurds

Lebanon
Pakistan
The Palestinians
Saudi Arabia
Syria
Turkey

KEY ICONS TO LOOK FOR:

 Words to Understand: These words with their easy-to-understand definitions will increase the reader's understanding of the text, while building vocabulary skills.

 Sidebars: This boxed material within the main text allows readers to build knowledge, gain insights, explore possibilities, and broaden their perspectives by weaving together additional information to provide realistic and holistic perspectives.

 Research Projects: Readers are pointed toward areas of further inquiry connected to each chapter. Suggestions are provided for projects that encourage deeper research and analysis.

 Text-Dependent Questions: These questions send the reader back to the text for more careful attention to the evidence presented there.

 Series Glossary of Key Terms: This back-of-the book glossary contains terminology used throughout this series. Words found here increase the reader's ability to read and comprehend higher-level books and articles in this field.

Introduction

by Camille Pecastaing, Ph.D.

Oil shocks, wars, terrorism, nuclear proliferation, military and autocratic regimes, ethnic and religious violence, riots and revolutions are the most frequent headlines that draw attention to the Middle East. The region is also identified with Islam, often in unflattering terms. The creed is seen as intolerant and illiberal, oppressive of women and minorities. There are concerns that violence is not only endemic in the region, but also follows migrants overseas. All clichés contain a dose of truth, but that truth needs to be placed in its proper context. The turbulences visited upon the Middle East that grab the headlines are only the symptoms of a deep social phenomenon: the demographic transition. This transition happens once in the life of a society. It is the transition from the agrarian to the industrial age, from rural to urban life, from illiteracy to mass education, all of which supported by massive population growth. It is this transition that fueled the recent development of East Asia, leading to rapid social and economic modernization and to some form of democratization there. It is the same transition that, back in the 19th century, inspired nationalism and socialism in Europe, and that saw the excesses of imperialism, fascism, and Marxist-Leninism. The demographic transition is a period of high risks and great opportunities, and the challenge for the Middle East is to fall on the right side of the sword.

In 1950, the population of the Middle East was about 100 million; it passed 250 million in 1990. Today it exceeds 400 million, to reach about 700 million by 2050. The growth of urbanization is rapid, and concentrated on the coasts and along the few rivers. 1950 Cairo, with an estimated population of 2.5 million, grew into Greater Cairo, a metropolis of about 18 million people. In the same period, Istanbul went from one to 14 million. This expanding populace was bound to test the social system, but regimes were unwilling to take chances with the private sector, reserving for the state a prominent place in the economy. That model failed, population grew faster than the economy, and stress fractures already appeared in the 1970s, with recurrent riots following IMF adjustment programs and the emergence of radical Islamist movements. Against a backdrop of military coups and social unrest, regimes consolidated their rule by subsidizing basic commodities, building up patronage networks (with massive under-employment in a non-productive public sector), and cementing autocratic practices. Decades of continuity in political elites between 1970 and 2010 gave the impression that they had succeeded. The Arab spring shattered that illusion.

The Arab spring exposed a paradox that the Middle East was both one, yet also diverse. Arab unity was apparent in the contagion: societies inspired other societies in a revolutionary wave that engulfed the region yet remained exclusive to it. The rebellious youth was the same; it watched the same footage on al Jazeera and turned to the same online social networks. The claims were the same: less corruption, less police abuse, better standards of living, and off with the tyrants. In some cases, the struggle was one: Syria became a global battlefield, calling young fighters from all around the region to a common cause. But there were differences in the way states fared during the Arab spring. Some escaped unscathed; some got by with a burst of public spending or a sprinkling of democratic reforms, and others yet collapsed into civil wars. The differential resilience of the regimes owes to both the strength and cohesiveness of the repressive apparatus, and the depth of the fiscal cushion they could tap into to buy social peace. Yemen, with a GDP per capita of $4000 and Qatar, at $94,000, are not the same animal. It also became apparent that, despite shared frustrations and a common cause, protesters and insurgents were extremely diverse.

Some embraced free-market capitalism, while others clamored for state welfare to provide immediate improvements to their standards of living. Some thought in terms of country, while other questioned that idea. The day after the Arab spring, everyone looked to democracy for solutions, but few were prepared to invest in the grind of democratic politics. It also quickly became obvious that the competition inherent in democratic life would tear at the social fabric. The few experiments with free elections exposed the formidable polarization between Islamists and non-Islamists. Those modern cleavages paralleled ancient but pregnant divisions. Under the Ottoman Millet system, ethnic and sectarian communities had for centuries coexisted in relative, self-governed segregation. Those communities remained a primary feature of social life, and in a dense, urbanized environment, fractures between Christians and Muslims, Shi'as and Sunnis, Arabs and Berbers, Turks and Kurds were combustible. Autocracy had kept the genie of divisiveness in the bottle. Democracy unleashed it.

This does not mean democracy has to forever elude the region, but that in countries where the state concentrates both political and economic power, elections are a polarizing zero-sum game—even more so when public patronage has to be cut back because of chronic budget deficits. The solution is to bring some distance between the state and the national economy. If all goes well, a growing private sector would absorb the youth, and generate taxes to balance state budgets. For that, the Middle East needs just enough democracy to mitigate endemic corruption, to protect citizens from abuse and extortion, and to allow greater transparency over public finances and over licensing to crony privateers.

Better governance is necessary but no sufficient. The region still needs to figure out a developmental model and find its niche in the global economy. Unfortunately, the timing is not favorable. Mature economies are slow growing, and emerging markets in Asia and Africa are generally more competitive than the Middle East. To succeed, the region has to leverage its assets, starting with its geographic location between Europe, Africa, and Asia. Regional businesses and governments are looking to anchor themselves in south-south relationships. They see the potential clientele of hundreds of millions in Africa and South Asia reaching middle class status, many of whom Muslim. The Middle East can also count on its vast sources of energy, and on the capital accumulated during years of high oil prices. Financial investments in specific sectors, like transport, have already made local companies like Emirates Airlines and DP World global players.

With the exception of Turkey and Israel, the weakness is human capital, which is either unproductive for lack of adequate education, or uncompetitive, because wage expectations in the region are relatively higher than in other emerging economies. The richer Arab countries have worked around the problem by importing low-skilled foreign labor—immigrants who notoriously toil for little pay and even less protection. In parallel, they have made massive investments in higher education, so that the productivity of their native workforce eventually reaches the compensations they expect. For lack of capital, the poorer Arab countries could not follow that route. Faced with low capitalization, sticky wages and high unemployment, they have instead allowed a shadow economy to grow. The arrangement keeps people employed, if at low levels of productivity, and in a manner that brings no tax revenue to the state.

Overall, the commerce of the region with the rest of the world is unhealthy. Oil exporters tend to be one-product economies highly vulnerable to fluctuations in global prices. Labor-rich countries depend too much on remittances from workers in the European Union and the oil-producing countries of the Gulf. Some of the excess labor has found employment in the jihadist sector, a high-risk but up and coming industry which pays decent salaries. For the poorer states of the region, jihadists are the ticket to foreign strategic rent. The Middle East got a taste for it in the early days of the Cold War, when either superpower provided aid to those who declared themselves in their camp. Since then, foreign strategic rent has come in many forms: direct military aid, preferential trade agreements, loan guarantees, financial assistance, or aid programs to cater to refugee populations. Rent never amounts to more than a few percentage points of GDP, but it is often enough to keep entrenched regimes in power. Dysfunction becomes self-perpetuating: pirates and jihadists, famine and refugees, all bear promises of aid to come from concerned distant powers. Reforms lose their urgency.

Turkey and Israel have a head start on the path to modernization and economic maturity, but they are, like the rest of the Middle East, consumed in high stakes politics that hinder their democratic life. Rather than being models that would lift others, they are virtually outliers disconnected from the rest of the region. The clock is ticking for the Middle East. The window of opportunity from the demographic transition will eventually close. Fertility is already dropping, and as the current youth bulge ages it will become a burden on the economy. The outlook for capital is also bleak. Oil is already running out for the smaller producers, all the while global prices are pushed downwards by the exploitation of new sources. The Middle East has a real possibility to break the patterns of the past, but the present is when the transition should occur.

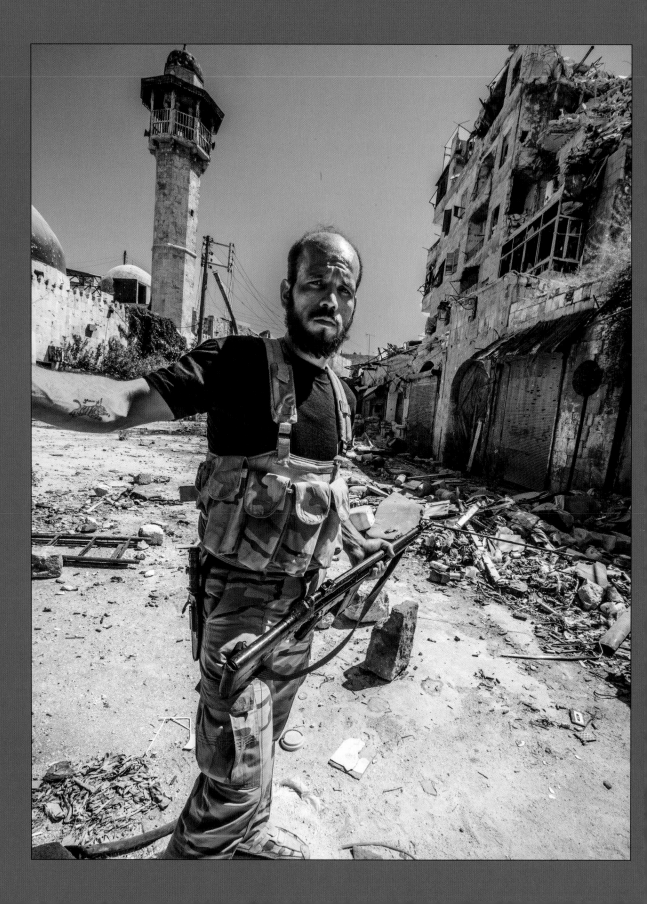

A member of the Free Syrian Army stands in a rebel-controlled area of Aleppo, Syria's largest city, in 2014. Since 2011, Syria has been engaged in a civil war between rebel and government forces. By February 2015, more than 220,000 people had been killed in the conflict.

Syria's Place in the World

I n March of 2011, a group of Syrian students was arrested in the southern city of Daraa for writing political graffiti on walls, including the statement "Down with the regime." The students were inspired by protests in other Middle Eastern countries that had begun a few months earlier, aimed at improving the political circumstances and living conditions of the Arab people.

It was perhaps not surprising that the Arab Spring protests should spread to the Syrian Arab Republic. It was also not surprising that the students would soon be arrested and jailed by Syrian authorities. Over the past 40 years, Syria has gained a reputation as one of the most repressive dictatorships in the world.

REPRESSIVE RULE IN SYRIA

Syria rests on the far eastern shore of the Mediterranean Sea in an region sometimes called the Levant, from a French word meaning "sunrise." To people in the Mediterranean region, the day dawns over Syria. And in many ways, the world we know today dawned in ancient Syria. This region was the site of much of the ancient world's traffic, as travelers frequently passed through going from one place to another. This position at the world's crossroads deeply influenced Syria's history and culture. Today, the remains of Syria's rich and glorious past can be seen in the ruins and archaeological sites throughout the country, which reveal layer after layer of civilization.

During the 1970s, a brutal dictator named Hafez al-Assad seized power in Syria through a **coup**. Once he gained power, Hafez al-Assad did not hesitate to use that power to crush anyone whom he thought posed a threat to his regime. For example, the Assad government responded to a 1982 protest in the city of Hama by sending in military troops who massacred approximately 25,000 civilians. Internationally, Assad joined Egypt in waging a surprise attack against Israel in October 1973, and sent Syrian troops to intervene in a civil war in neighboring Lebanon in 1976; those troops allowed Syria to effectively control Lebanon for the next three decades. Syria's poor human-rights record, as well as its support for terrorist organizations led the United States to break off diplomatic relations, impose **economic sanctions**, and list the country as a "state sponsor of terrorism" in 1979.

Words to Understand in This Chapter

coup—short for coup d'etat, the sudden illegal overthrow of one government for another, usually by means of force.

economic sanctions—penalties imposed by one country on another, in an effort to weaken the economy of the targeted nation. This, it is hoped, will make the targeted country change policies or behaviors that are considered undesirable or detrimental to the targeting nation.

Children in the village of Kahnsheikhoun lay flowers on the grave of a friend who was killed by government fire during the civil war.

When Hafez al-Assad died in 2000, power passed to his son, Bashar al-Assad, a British-educated ophthalmologist who had no previous governing experience. Many Syrians hoped that Bashar would be open to political reforms that would provide greater freedom, and the new president himself spoke of permitting greater democracy. Yet those hopes were not realized. In 2010, the international watchdog agency Freedom House continued to rank Syria among the "least free" countries of the world.

Supporters of Bashar al-Assad argue the fractured nature of Syrian society requires such repressive measures. The Assad family are members of a Muslim religious sect known as the Alawi, which are a minority in the country. Sunni Muslims make up around 74 percent of the population, with Shiite Muslims and the

Bashar al-Assad has been president of Syria since 2000. Initially, Syrians believed he might be a more liberal ruler than his father, but Bashar implemented practically no political reforms in his first decade in power. The Syrian civil war began as a protest against his authoritarian rule.

Alawi making up 13 percent; Arab Christians 10 percent; and a group called the Druze making up another 3 percent. In addition, Syria's population includes Arabs, Kurds, Armenians, and other ethnic groups. The borders of present-day Syria were set in the 1920s, and Syria did not become an independent country until the 1940s. Many people feel more loyal to their family, tribal, religious, or ethnic group than they do to the idea of the Syrian nation.

OUTBREAK OF CIVIL WAR

In March 2011, the Syrian government responded to the anti-regime graffiti in a typical way—by arresting and torturing the students involved. This sparked nation-wide demonstrations, and escalated into an armed conflict that has taken more than 220,000 lives and displaced more than 9 million people, roughly half of Syria's population.

Many rebel groups emerged to oppose the Bashar al-Assad government. One of the first was the Free Syrian Army, composed mostly of former Syrian military officers and soldiers. The Free Syrian Army captured most of Aleppo, Syria's second-largest city, in 2012. The Free Syrian Army is largely secular, but a number of other rebel groups were driven by Islamist ideology. These groups want to see the replacement of worldly governments with a theocracy that rules in accordance with Islamic laws and principles.

Among the most notable of these Islamist groups is the Islamic State of Iraq and the Levant (ISIL), which by the summer of 2014 had gained control over more than one-third of Syria's territory, as well as large areas of Iraq. On June 29, 2014, ISIL's leaders declared that the group had established a caliphate that would henceforth have religious, political, and military authority over all Muslims throughout the world.

ISIL is not the only Islamist group fighting in Syria; others include the Army of Mujahedeen and the Islamic Front, as well as a branch of the international terrorist organization al-Qaeda that is known in Syria as the al-Nusra Front. While all share a common goal of overthrowing the Assad regime, these Islamist groups have fought each other, and have also clashed with the Free Syrian Army and other rebel groups.

The civil war in Syria threatens to destabilize the entire Middle East, one of the world's most strategically important regions due to its vast reserves of oil, as well as its history in the establishment and practice of three of the world's major religions. Syria can't afford continuous warfare for much longer, but it remains uncertain whether the Assad government can make peace on its own terms, or will be overthrown and replaced by something else.

 Text-Dependent Questions

1. Where is the Levant? What does the word *Levant* mean?
2. What rebel group gained control over the city of Aleppo in 2012?

 Research Project

In Islam, a caliphate is a theocratic state in which the ruler (known as a caliph), has authority over both the spiritual and temporal lives of his subjects and all people must obey Islamic laws. The organization ISIL has declared that it is forming a new caliphate, to which all Muslims must pledge allegiance. Find a world map online, and identify the ten countries with the greatest population of Muslims (Indonesia, Pakistan, India, Bangladesh, Egypt, Nigeria, Iran, Turkey, Algeria, and Morocco. How close are these countries to the lands where ISIL holds territory (Iraq and Syria)?

The Euphrates River, one of three major waterways that run through Syria, flows past ancient fortifications near the village of Halabia.

The Land

I n ancient times, Syria's land nurtured the growth of civilization and the birth of farming. Today, managing the land is a major challenge. Loss of forestland, soil erosion, low water levels, and a growing desert threaten to make Syria's land unaccommodating for its growing population.

A good portion of Syria's terrain is **steppe** or desert. The steppe spreads across the country's northern region, which shares a border with Turkey; the Syrian Desert, which is expanding, lies in the southeastern region, stretching into Jordan and Iraq. Other forms of terrain in Syria include a long coastal plain running along the Mediterranean Sea, and two mountain ranges, both of which run north to south in the western part of the country.

With desert and steppe so prominent in Syria, a dry climate is found throughout most areas of the country. Only about 25 percent of Syria's land area is suitable for farming. **Irrigation** from Syria's two primary rivers makes agriculture possible on 3,500 square miles (9,061 square kilometers), a small portion of the country's total area of 71,508 square miles (185,180 sq km). These rivers are the Orontes in the west, which flows north into the Mediterranean, and the Euphrates in the east, which flows northwest to southeast through Turkey, Syria, and Iraq.

The rest of Syria's farmland depends on rain to water crops. Some regions receive good amounts of rain in the winter, particularly along the coast and in certain parts of the mountain ranges. In those mountainous areas, the winter can be too cold to support a year-round growing season. Conversely, Syria's summers can be too hot and dry for farmland that relies on rainfall. In grassy areas of the steppe and in the mountains, the soil is often too poor to support farming. However, there is enough grass and foliage to nourish flocks of sheep and other animals. Forty-three percent of Syria's land is used as pasture for animals to graze.

Although sheep are fairly abundant in Syria, along with other agricultural and pack animals such as cattle, camels, goats, horses, and chickens, wildlife is scarce. Wild animals have been hunted and their habitats destroyed for thousands of years in Syria, at such a rate that today very few remain.

THE COASTAL REGION

Blessed with rich, red soil and a moist Mediterranean climate, Syria's short, narrow coastal strip has the most fertile farmland in

Words to Understand in This Chapter

irrigation—the process of bringing water to an agricultural land from a distant water source via canals and ditches.

steppe—level, treeless, grassy plains with low rainfall, found in eastern Europe and Asia.

Syria is mountainous along the coasts and in the southern part of the country. Major waterways include the Euphrates, Khabur, and Orontes rivers. Lake Al-Asad was created when a dam was built across the Euphrates River in the 1970s; the dam's hydroelectric plants produce more than 70 percent of Syria's electricity. Water from Lake Al-Asad is also used to irrigate fields, as well as to provide drinking water for residents of Syria's largest city, Aleppo.

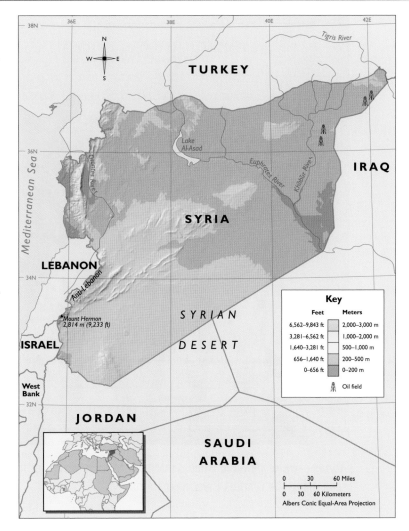

the country. Along its entire 120-mile (193-km) stretch, there is no point that is more than 20 miles (32 km) wide. A chain of rocky, limestone mountains, the Nusayriyah, divides the coast from the rest of the country and prevents most of the Mediterranean's moisture from reaching the interior. This area receives more rain than the rest of the country, about 30 to 40 inches (76 to 102 centimeters) per year. Rain falls almost entirely between October and March, with the largest amount falling in January. Although it rarely rains in the summer, the humidity is very high throughout the season.

Norias—water-powered wheels intended to raise water for irrigation purposes—can still be seen along the Orontes River near Hama.

Thanks to the sea, the coastal climate is mild. It is cooler in the summer and warmer in the winter than elsewhere in Syria. The average temperature in summer is 84° Fahrenheit (29° Celsius) on the coast, compared to 90°F (32°C) and higher in the capital city, Damascus. The mild climate makes year-round farming and cultivating possible in the coastal region. Olive groves, vegetable gardens, and fruit-tree orchards are the most common commercial ventures. Citrus trees, corn, and sunflowers all grow well in this region. Hedges of cypress trees divide the fields and shield the crops from winds blowing in from the Mediterranean.

MOUNTAIN RANGES

The Nusayriyah Mountains (Jabal an-Nusayriyah) hug the Syrian coastline, stretching from the Turkish border in the north into Lebanon in the south. They are about 40 miles (64 km) wide, with their peaks averaging 4,000 feet (1,220 meters) above sea level. These mountains grow higher farther to the south, reaching their maximum height in Lebanon.

Once covered in trees, these mountains are no longer heavily wooded. The little forestland that remains in Syria is located here, with cool groves of evergreen trees gracing the lower western slopes. Moisture from the Mediterranean is trapped by the steep mountains, depositing 40 to 50 inches (101 to 127 cm) of rain on the western slopes of the mountains every year. Many of the forests

 Quick Facts: The Geography of Syria

Location: Middle East, bordering the Mediterranean Sea, between Lebanon and Turkey
Area: slightly larger than North Dakota
    total: 71,508 square miles (185,180 sq km)
    land: 71,062 square miles (184,050 sq km)
    water: 436 square miles (1,130 sq km)
Borders: Iraq 376 miles (605 km), Israel 47 miles (76 km), Jordan 233 miles (375 km), Lebanon 233 miles (375 km), Turkey 511 miles (822 km), coastline 120 miles (193 km)
Climate: mostly desert; hot, dry, sunny summers (June to August) and mild, rainy winters (December to February) along coast; cold weather with snow or sleet periodically in Damascus
Terrain: primarily semiarid and desert plateau; narrow coastal plain; mountains in west
Elevation extremes:
    lowest point: unnamed location near Lake Tiberias—656 feet (200 meters) below sea level
    highest point: Mount Hermon—9,232 feet (2,814 meters)
Natural hazards: dust storms, sandstorms

Source: CIA World Factbook, 2015.

The fertile area south of Mount Hermon, known as the Golan Heights, has been occupied by Israel since 1967.

have disappeared because farmers have planted orchards in the hopes of taking advantage of the area's abundant rainfall. The eastern slopes and the lands beyond them receive very little of this rain, making them suitable only for grazing.

The Nusayriyah Mountains are difficult to cross, but a valley opens up just west of the city of Homs. Roads through the Homs

Gap link Homs to the city of Tripoli on the Lebanese coast. Oil pipelines also travel through the gap, bringing oil from Syria and Iraq to the coast where it can be sold to other countries. To the east of the mountains, the Orontes River flows northward from its source in the Lebanese Mountains, dumping into the Mediterranean in Turkey near the Syrian border. The Orontes Valley is bounded by the Nusayriyah range to the west and the Anti-Lebanon Mountains to the east. It is one of the most heavily populated industrial and agricultural regions in the country.

Two of Syria's largest cities, Homs and Hama, lie along the Orontes, opposite the Syrian coast on the other side of the Nusayriyah range. Damascus, the capital of Syria, lies at the foot of these mountains on a narrow strip of steppe facing the Syrian Desert. Rainfall here is sparse and unpredictable with frequent droughts. Damascus often receives as little as 7 inches (18 cm) of rain in a year. A number of underground springs water an area near Damascus known as the Ghouta oasis, where fruit orchards are abundant. Flowing into the Ghouta from the mountains is the Barada River, which has enabled Damascus to prosper since ancient times.

Syria's other major mountain range, the Anti-Lebanon Mountains, lie to the east of the Orontes River. In the south, the peaks of the Anti-Lebanon form the border between Lebanon and Syria, with Lebanon lying to the west. The highest point in Syria, Mount Hermon, is in the southern part of this range near Syria's border with Israel. The eastern slopes of the Anti-Lebanon Mountains receive very little rain, and the barren Syrian Desert takes hold of the land south and east of the moun-

 Did You Know?

An oasis is a fertile area in the desert that receives water from underground springs. Settlements and cities in the desert are usually built on oases.

A shepherd's hut surrounded by rocky terrain. Most of Syria is arid steppe or dry desert, and in many areas the land is more suited for grazing animals than for farming.

tains, continuing all the way to the borders of Jordan and Iraq.

The area south of Mount Hermon is a fertile area known as the Golan Heights, which Israel has occupied since June 1967. Many streams from the mountains provide the area with ample water. One-third of Israel's water supply originates in the Golan. Since the 1960s, there has been an ongoing international conflict over the management of the Yarmouk River, which begins in Syria, then flows along the Syrian-Jordanian border until reaching the Jordan River in Israel. The Yarmouk is the largest tributary to the Jordan, from which Israel and Jordan draw large amounts of water. Israel has often clashed with Syria over the amount of water Syria has taken from the Yarmouk. Jordan has also been in conflict with

Syria over its use of the river, most heatedly during drought periods. The region's countries have yet to reach a permanent agreement over their shared water resources.

STEPPE AND DESERT

East of the Anti-Lebanon Mountains, a narrow strip of steppe in the south widens as it stretches north. This steppe covers the entire northern area of Syria, and to the far north it meets the Taurus Mountains in Turkey. Desert covers the area to the east and south of the steppe. Most of the rain in the steppe falls in the winter. Although temperatures can plunge below freezing, winters are generally mild. The winter rains make it possible to grow wheat without irrigation. Aleppo, Syria's second-largest city, lies in the

The ruins of a Roman city rise from the desert near Palmyra.

western part of this steppe region. It receives about 18 inches (45.5 cm) of rain annually. The summers here are very hot and dry. Grasses, clover, and small shrubs that grow on the steppe make it ideal grazing land for animals.

The large, sparsely populated desert of Syria is very rocky with little natural wildlife or vegetation. The bit of scrub that grows there during the winter months dries up as the hot, dry summer progresses. The heat and dryness increase as one goes farther south and east. About 5 inches (12.7 cm) of rain falls on the desert annually. The region can experience extreme cold as well as heat. Typically, daytime temperatures in the summer range from 90°F to 100°F (32°C to 38°C), but people have reported temperatures as high as 120°F (49°C).

At the southwestern end of the Syrian Desert lies a range of extinct volcanoes called the Jebel Arab, formerly called the Jebel Druz. The plateau north and west of the Jebel Arab is called the Hauran. It is dotted with fertile patches of volcanic soil in between stretches of basalt, which is black rock created by lava flows. Many springs in the area provide water for agriculture, and the land produces a considerable amount of wheat. In addition to receiving water from these springs, the area annually collects about 24 inches (61 cm) of rain arriving from the coast. Many ruins dating back to the Bronze Age and earlier periods reveal that the area has been settled and cultivated since ancient times. Many ancient buildings, as well as modern structures, are composed of the basalt common to the region.

VALLEYS AND PLAINS

The Euphrates River divides the northeast corner of Syria from the rest of the country. The Euphrates flows from Turkey into the Syrian steppe in the north and continues south and east through the desert into Iraq. Dams in Turkey, Syria, and Iraq regulate the river's flow. Two tributaries, the Balikh and the Khabur, are major rivers that flow north from the Euphrates.

Hydroelectric plants on these dams have helped Turkey, Syria, and Iraq bring electricity to more areas. Until dams were built, it was difficult to divert the water of the Euphrates from its deep gorge to farmland on the higher plane surrounding it. But, in a situation similar to that in Syria, Israel, and Jordan, dams and irrigation canals in Syria draw water away from the next user downstream, Iraq. With water a scarce and precious resource in this part of the region, the use of the Euphrates has been a subject of ongoing dispute among Syria, Turkey, and Iraq.

The northeast corner of Syria beyond the Euphrates is called the Jazira Plain. Rivers in the region provide the land with a good supply of water for irrigation farming. Until recently, the sparsely populated Jazira has been mostly grassland. Sources of irrigation combined with good rainfall have raised hopes that the Jazira will become a highly productive agricultural region. The discovery of oil in the Jazira has also sparked the interest of investors from Syria and neighboring countries.

 # Text-Dependent Questions

1. Which two large Syrian cities are located on the Orontes River?
2. What mountain is the highest point in Syria? Where is it located?
3. During what season does rain fall in the steppe areas of Syria?

 # Research Project

The Euphrates River, which flows through Syria, is one of the longest and most historically important rivers of the Middle East region. Using an atlas from your school library, or a reputable Internet source, find out more about the history of human development along the Euphrates, as well as the local flora and fauna found there. Create a poster (or an electronic slideshow) with pictures of the river, villages or settlements along it, and fish, animals, and plants that are found in it. In a few paragraphs, include details about the river, such as its length, average volume, speed of water flow, and other interesting information.

The area today known as Syria was home to some of the earliest human civilizations. In Palmyra, located in the southeastern part of the country, are the remains of a temple of Baal. This was the name given to various gods worshiped by ancient people of the Middle East before the emergence of the three monotheistic religions that would reshape the region—Judaism, Christianity, and Islam.

History

Many Westerners are familiar with some aspects of Syria's ancient history through the people, places, and events of the Bible, as many biblical events occurred in or near the region of modern-day Syria. The area's original inhabitants were nomadic tribes that followed their flocks of sheep and goats from place to place in search of food and water. These people belonged to a group known as the **Semites**. They spoke a number of related Semitic languages. A small number of Syrians today still live much as these early nomads did thousands of years ago.

Syria's location has greatly helped shape its history. As a crossroads of the ancient world, it is a link between the Mediterranean cultures of the west and the civilizations of the Far East in Persia (now called Iran), India, and China. Historians and archaeologists have long believed that humans first began to live in settled communities and farm the land in Mesopotamia, an area along the Euphrates River in the modern-day country of Iraq. Remains of ancient cities found in Syria reveal that it, too, was home to some of the earliest human civilizations.

Throughout most of Syria's history, the land has been ruled by one empire or another. Family and tribal ties have always been more important than government allegiance to people in this area of the world. A local tribal chief was often a more powerful figure to the local people than a distant emperor, though when an empire was at the height of its power, citizens were more likely to enjoy more stability, as they lived in organized settlements and cultivated the land with few hindrances.

Syria's location was its greatest attraction to the ruling empires. One of the main routes between the Far East and the

 Words to Understand in This Chapter

armistice—an agreement between two warring parties to stop fighting.

caliph—the title of a successor of Muhammad as the spiritual and political leader of Islam.

caravan—a train of pack animals carrying cargo from one place to another.

diplomatic relations—a relationship between two countries in which each agrees to acknowledge the independent statehood of the other and establish ties through government representatives known as diplomats.

embassy—the official headquarters of an ambassador and his or her staff.

imams—leaders of prayer in a Muslim mosque, also those descendants of Muhammad's cousin Ali believed by Shiite Muslims to be Islam's legitimate rulers.

League of Nations—an organization of nations that lasted from 1920 to 1946.

mandates—orders to act that are given to representatives; specifically the authority given by the League of Nations that its member nations administer and establish a government on a conquered territory.

martial law—law that is enforced by military power, usually in a state of emergency when the civilian government is unable to keep order.

monotheism—belief in the existence of only one God.

Semites—people of the Eastern Mediterranean area descended from its original Semitic tribes, including Jews and Arabs.

Mediterranean Sea was along overland ***caravan*** trails. Goods from China and India were carried to the Mediterranean coast on pack animals that had to cross the Syrian Desert. Cities along the trade routes, such as Latakia, Damascus, and Palmyra, eventually became major trading centers.

The first empires to conquer Syria came from Mesopotamia in the east. Later, Egypt and other ancient empires would control the region as well. In 332 BCE the Macedonian conqueror Alexander the Great conquered Syria. During the centuries after Alexander's conquests, Syria and the Middle East were greatly influenced by Greek culture.

The Roman general Pompey invaded and conquered the area in 64 BCE, and Syria became a

 Did You Know?

The Phoenicians lived on the Syrian coast during the first millennium BCE. They developed the oldest alphabet that has ever been discovered. The Greeks developed their alphabet through contact with the Phoenicians. The Romans took the concept from the Greeks and passed it on to those who developed the modern system of the 26-letter alphabet.

province of Rome. At this time the Roman Empire was enjoying a period of expansion and great wealth, and it benefited greatly from the caravans that passed through the major Syrian trade centers.

The Roman era was a time of religious as well as economic change. Christianity was born under Roman rule in the Jewish communities of Jerusalem and Galilee. During the first and second centuries of the common era (CE), Antioch and Damascus became important centers of early Christianity. A Jewish leader named Saul had a miraculous encounter with Jesus Christ while traveling to Damascus. After converting to the Christian faith and taking the new name of Paul, he preached Christianity while traveling through Syria and the neighboring regions of the Middle East and southern Europe. Paul also wrote many epistles, which later became part of the biblical New Testament.

The ruins of a Byzantine cathedral which was built in the fifth century CE. Syria was an important center of the early Christian church, with several apostles establishing churches there during the first and second centuries.

From the cities of Palestine, the religion eventually spread across the entire Roman Empire. The Roman emperor Constantine converted to Christianity in the fourth century CE. In CE 330 he moved the capital of the empire from Rome to the Greek city of Byzantium in modern-day Turkey. While Constantinople (as it was renamed) established itself as the new capital, Christianity became the state religion in Syria and the other Roman provinces. In the early fifth century, the western Roman Empire collapsed but the eastern part of the empire survived as the Byzantine Empire. For over two more centuries, Syria remained a vital center of Christianity, and a great deal of Greek and Roman culture and learning was preserved in Syrian monasteries.

Schisms eventually developed among Christians in this region. A sect called the Monophysites, established in the fifth century, proclaimed the wholly divine nature of Jesus Christ. At the Council of Chalcedon in 451, church leaders formulated an orthodox doctrine that argued for the dual nature of Christ as both human and divine being. The Monophysites, most prominent in Egypt, Syria, and Armenia, rejected the orthodox beliefs endorsed by the Council of Chalcedon. Thus developed a number of alternative sects whose descendants in present-day Syria are the Armenian Orthodox and Syrian Orthodox churches. The split that was led by the Monophysites left the Christian forces more vulnerable to foreign threats, as the Muslim conquests later demonstrated.

THE BIRTH OF ISLAM AND THE MUSLIM CONQUEST

Around 570, a man named Muhammad was born in Mecca, a town of merchants situated on a caravan route in the Arabian Peninsula. In a very short time, Muhammad would found another religion that would change the Middle East forever.

Muhammad is considered the last of the prophets by his followers, who are called Muslims. The religion Muhammad founded is known as Islam, and he was its spiritual, political, and military leader. Islam soon spread across the entire Arabian Peninsula. Arab Muslims moved quickly to conquer other people and spread their new religion. As the Arabs moved north into Syria, the Byzantines could not withstand them. The Arabs captured Damascus in 635, only a few years after the death of Muhammad. Because the region's Christians were suffering a lack of unity, the Muslim occupation met with little resistance, and much of Syria's population converted to Islam during the next few centuries.

Nonetheless, Christianity had a stronger foundation in Syria than in other Muslim-dominated territories, and some sects survived the conquest in small numbers. Their staying power owed much to the Judeo-Christian tradition's affinity with Islam and its **monotheism**. Syria thus enjoyed a moderate level of coexistence between the Christians and the Muslim authorities. However, Christians were prohibited from spreading their faith, and since then have remained the religious minority in Syria.

After Muhammad died, his followers chose a successor and gave him the title of **caliph**. The caliph took Muhammad's place as the religious and political leader of all Muslims. Thirty years after Muhammad's death, a serious disagreement over the leadership of Islam developed in the Muslim community. One group, who came to be known as Sunnis, supported the caliph chosen by the Muslim leaders. Others, who came to be known as Shiites, believed that the leaders of Islam should follow the bloodline stemming from Muhammad's cousin and son-in-law, Ali. These particular leaders are called **imams**.

The Sunni caliph founded the Omayyad dynasty, which ruled from Damascus for about 90 years. Arab Islamic rule spread across North Africa and Spain to the west and as far as western India to the east under the Omayyads. The Omayyads were overthrown in 750 and a new caliphate, the Abbasid, established itself at Baghdad in Iraq.

Islamic culture soared to new heights during this time, while Europe, recovering from the fall of the Roman Empire, experienced a great decline. The Muslims' achievements in medicine, science, and mathematics surpassed most achievements of past cultures. Unlike the ancient Greek scientists, whose ideas were mainly theo-retical, the Muslims relied on hands-on experimentation and obser-vation. Algebra was invented under Muslim rule, and a vaccine for smallpox was developed long before it was discovered in the West.

In the 10th century, warlike Turks converted to Islam in great numbers, though they continued speaking their native language, Turkish, instead of switching to Arabic like other converts had done. They began to migrate westward, and in 1055, a group of invaders captured Baghdad. The leader of the Turks, Tughril Beg, assumed the title of sultan, but allowed the serving caliph to remain as spiritual leader.

European Christians grew concerned as the Muslim Turks moved closer to Constantinople. Across Europe and the Middle East, European kings launched a series of battle campaigns called the Crusades. On the European fronts, the kings sought to clean out the areas plagued by marauders and bandits. In the Middle East, they wanted to wrest Palestine from Muslim control as well as take over Constantinople. The Crusaders succeeded in capturing Jerusalem in 1099 and the Syrian coast in the following years. They built castles and fortresses in Syria's western mountains to defend

The Crusades were a series of wars fought between 1096 and 1291, during which European Christians attempted to gain control of sites they considered holy in Palestine and Syria. This castle was built by Crusaders near Aleppo in the 12th century. Today, it is a UNESCO World Heritage Site, and is considered one of the best preserved Medieval castles.

their holdings. The brutality of the Crusaders toward their enemies convinced many Syrian Christians to convert to Islam.

During the late Middle Ages, Europe began to emerge from the ignorance that had long enveloped it. Culture and thought began to flourish again as the achievements of the Greeks and the Romans were rediscovered. Sailors from Portugal, taking advantage of advances in sailing and navigation, explored the world and discovered alternative ocean routes to India. These routes were faster, cheaper, and less cumbersome than the old caravan trails passing through the Middle East. In the centuries ahead, developments in technology, trade, and military warfare enabled European powers to continually gain greater control over the affairs of the Middle East.

OTTOMAN AND EUROPEAN RULE

During the 14th century, the Ottoman Turks came to power in Anatolia, north of Syria. In 1453 the Turks captured Constantinople from the Byzantines, a feat that stunned and delighted the Muslim world. Once the Ottomans established Constantinople (renamed Istanbul) as their capital, they began to conquer Arab lands to the south. They captured Syria in 1516.

By the 16th century, the Ottoman Empire extended across North Africa, east to Iran, into the Arabian Peninsula, down both shores of the Red Sea, north to all the areas surrounding the Black Sea, and west into Europe's Balkan Peninsula. Syria was ruled from Constantinople and became a backwater, isolated from the capital and receiving little of the central government's attention.

As devout Muslims, the Ottomans were deeply committed to putting the world under Islamic rule. Under Sultan Suleyman the Magnificent, they turned their attention to the west. When his troops attacked Vienna in 1529, it looked as though Suleyman was on the brink of capturing the heart of Europe. But the Turks did not take Vienna from the Habsburgs of Austria. In 1683 the

Ottoman Turks tried again to invade Europe, but were stopped once more at Vienna.

From the birth of Islam until 1683, Muslim rulers had successfully conquered nearly every land in their sights. Muslims viewed themselves as a superior civilization with a mission to spread Allah's truth throughout the world. But the tide began to turn against them, as the Ottoman Empire eventually proved to be more vulnerable than it originally thought.

Even as the Ottoman Empire threatened Europe, its power was being threatened by European technology, naval power, and commerce. After centuries of conquest, the Ottomans now had to defend what they conquered. The Europeans

The reign of Sultan Suleyman I between 1520 and 1566 is generally regarded as the high point of the Ottoman Empire. Suleyman (known as "the Magnificent" and "the Lawgiver") expanded the Ottoman Empire into eastern Europe, the Arabian Peninsula, and along the Mediterranean. Greater Syria had fallen under Ottoman control in 1516.

began to recover the lands they had lost and ultimately took over the Ottomans' territory around the Black Sea and in North Africa.

The Ottomans struggled to defend themselves against the dominant European militaries, particularly the naval forces. West Europeans had learned to build large, powerful ships that could withstand the rough seas of the Atlantic Ocean. For the Europeans, owning the seas soon meant owning most of the world as they began to conquer and colonize far-flung areas. The people of the Middle East had reaped the benefits from their location as the gateway to China and India. But when Europeans began traveling to the Far East on the ocean, the desert routes continually saw less traffic, and the world's trade began to neglect the Middle East.

The sultan's government was also losing strength in relation to the governments of Europe. European countries were developing strong central governments that could draw on all their countries' resources to coordinate war and trade. In contrast, the Ottoman government was less centralized and its local governors beyond Constantinople and Anatolia were losing control of their provinces.

In most of the outlying provinces, the sultan appointed governors known as *pashas* and transferred most government power to them. The *pashas* were given land and the task of collecting taxes for the sultan in return for military service. They took on increasing powers in their local areas, including raising troops for defense and keeping order. Many subjects of the sultan had almost no contact with his government throughout their entire lives. They paid taxes but received no government protection or services. They eventually grew more defiant. During this period, the provinces also suffered from the repeated invasions of central Asians. These invasions date back to as early as 1260, when much of Damascus and Aleppo were destroyed by Mongol conquerors.

During the 18th century, the Ottomans slowly realized they were failing to compete with Europe's growing wealth and technology. They began seeking alliances with West European countries to help protect them from Austria-Hungary and Russia threatening them from the north and east. The Ottomans purchased weapons and ships from Europeans. They also began employing them to train and advise their troops, and even commissioned some to serve as officers in the Ottoman army.

As a result of accepting European assistance, the Ottomans lost much of their power and autonomy. The stage was now set for the hungry powers of Europe to eventually take over Ottoman territory. At first, countries invaded not with guns, but with money. The Ottomans waged wars with Russia and other neighbors to the east that they couldn't win alone. Once again, they could not refuse the European offers of aid. In exchange for that aid, they were obligated to sign treaties granting European investors rights in their territories—rights that many of their own subjects didn't have. Foreigners could conduct business in Ottoman territory with few restrictions while paying lower taxes than Ottoman subjects paid. Europeans eventually owned most of the businesses and all of the banks in the empire.

During the late 19th century, Britain withdrew the support it had been giving to the Ottomans. At this point, Germany stepped in to fill the void and began offering military aid. German archaeologists began to explore the Middle East, and ground was broken for a railroad connecting Berlin to the Persian Gulf. When World War I broke out in Europe in 1914, the Ottoman government entered the war as a German ally.

By siding with the Germans, the Ottomans found themselves fighting against Great Britain, France, and Russia. Until this point, Britain and France had been trying to keep the Ottoman government strong so that it could impede the advances of Russia. By World War I, however, they believed the empire was going to collapse anyway and began plotting to take over Ottoman territories after the war. Britain and France negotiated the Sykes-Picot Agreement, which outlined a plan for dividing the Arab lands of the Middle East between them. The plan also stated that the two countries would consult with Italy and Russia about land claims they might have. The governments approved the agreement in January 1916, but they kept it secret until the new Russian communist government disclosed the plan in October of the following year.

Europe also became involved in the Middle East in hopes of settling the issue of the Jews. A number of British politicians were supporters of Zionism, a Jewish movement that championed the creation of a Jewish national homeland in Palestine. Though some

Jews had lived in Palestine since ancient times, after CE 135 most Jewish people been forced to live in scattered settlements all over Europe and Asia. They had often suffered persecution and discrimination in European countries. In the middle of the 19th century, some European Jews began moving to Palestine to escape this persecution. By World War I, they formed a sizable minority near the coast in the southern part of the Ottoman Empire's Syrian territory. In 1917, the British government issued the Balfour Declaration, a pledge of support for a national Jewish home.

In the meantime, Britain had begun to encourage the disgruntled Arabs to revolt against the Ottoman government. The British were hoping the Arabs would join the war on their side, giving them a large fighting force in the Middle East. The emir of Mecca, Sharif Hussein bin Ali, did lead a revolt against the Ottomans, although the Arab world did not unite under him as the British had anticipated.

An Arab fighting force, led by Hussein's son Faisal, joined the British. British and Arab troops captured Damascus from the Ottomans in 1918. As military governor, Faisal claimed control of much of Syria, and made preparations to establish a new state. On October 30, 1918, the Ottomans and the British signed an *armistice* agreement. It allowed the Ottomans to keep their Turkish territory, but all the Arab territory was divided between Britain and France as part of the *mandates* enacted by the *League of Nations*, an international organization that arose from the peace treaties ending World War I. In 1920, the French army occupied Damascus and turned out Faisal, who had been proclaimed king earlier that year.

Under the terms of the League of Nations mandates, Britain would control Iraq and a part of southern Syria, which was then called Transjordan; France would control northern Syria, as well as Greater Lebanon. This area centered around the Christian community on Mount Lebanon, to which the French added a good part of the seacoast. The mandates gave Britain and France the authority to manage these areas of the Middle East until the inhabitants were ready to govern themselves. The Balfour Declaration, with its support for a Jewish homeland, was written into the mandate for Palestine.

Britain decided that the Jordan River would separate Transjordan in the east and Palestine in the west. The British government aimed to set up constitutional monarchies modeled on its own government, planning after 1920 for Faisal to be king of Iraq and his brother Abdullah to be king of Transjordan. These monarchies turned out to be more authoritarian than what the British expected of a typical constitutional monarchy. Britain opted for direct control of Palestine instead of setting up a local government, and made initial plans to turn Palestine into the Jewish

Officers of the French military garrison in Damascus stand at attention. France ruled the area from 1920 until 1946; the League of Nations officially gave France control of Syria and Lebanon in 1922.

homeland promised by the Balfour Declaration.

The French created a republic in Lebanon. An area of the Mediterranean coast containing the cities of Antioch and Alexandretta (now called Iskenderun) received special status because it possessed a large Turkish minority. In 1938, the French gave this land to the Turks, and it became the Hatay province.

Although there had never really been a fully realized Syrian state to divide, many people of the Greater Syrian region deeply resented what they saw as the carving up of their homeland. They were especially angry at the loss of their seacoast to Lebanon and Turkey. Equally disturbing was that the French government treated Syria like a colony, rather than as a country that would one day rule itself. In the schools, French was the language used in the classrooms, and the French national anthem was sung every day.

Syrian nationalist leaders salute their supporters from the balcony of a building in Damascus, March 1936. Rioting broke out in Syria after the French government banished the nationalists to the desert near Deir el-Zor. To stop the violence, the French commissioner of Syria granted amnesty to the exiled nationalists and political prisoners. In the years between the first and second World Wars, most Syrians resented the French presence in their homeland.

Syrians railed against these attempts to force them to become French. It was clear to them that the French policies in Syria were for the benefit of France, not the Syrian people.

Because they were so resented, the French needed the threat of force to stay in power, and so they held onto firm control of the military. They encouraged minorities to join the military, believing they would be more loyal to the French than Sunni Muslims. Throughout Syria's history, the Druze and the Alawi religious minorities had been isolated from the mainstream population; with the French military they found opportunities that they had not had before. The local French armed forces, the Troupes Speciales du Levant, were staffed with French officers and local troops. Syrian Christians, some of whom stemmed from a line of Christians left behind by the Crusades, also found favor with the French and moved up through the ranks.

In the years following the the First World War, Syrian nationalism became a growing force, especially among educated young people in Damascus. Syrian nationalists began to demand a voice in government, and protests became more common. In 1928, France allowed the formation of the Nationalist Bloc, which folded several nationalist groups into one organization. Many of the conservative landowning families, realizing they had to protect their interests in the political process, joined the alliance. The Nationalist Bloc wrote a constitution for Syria, but France only agreed to it in 1930 after eliminating the articles that made Syria an independent nation. This modified constitution created a government made up of Syrians, though the French still held the real power.

In 1939, France finalized an agreement with Turkey and ceded the Alexandretta area to Turkey, removing yet another piece of Syria's shrunken coastline. Syrians were outraged. In the uprisings that followed, France established **martial law** and dissolved Syria's parliament. Once again, Syrians had no voice in government.

WORLD WAR II AND INDEPENDENCE

In September 1939, World War II broke out in Europe. France was quickly overwhelmed and surrendered to Nazi Germany in June 1940. A new French government was set up in the city of Vichy. The Vichy government, which controlled Syria and other French colonies, collaborated with the Nazis. In London, a provisional resistance government called Free France formed under Charles de Gaulle, with plans to continue fighting the Germans and liberate France. De Gaulle petitioned for Syria's military assistance, in return for which he promised Syria's eventual independence. Syria believed that it could further its own goals by entering the war. In 1943 Vichy France still had the Troupes Speciales du Levant in place, but the Nationalist Bloc defied them by declaring the French mandate over. They also elected a parliament and a president, Shukri al-Quwatli. By 1945, Syria had formed a national army and joined Free France and the other Allies in the war.

After the end of the war, a new international organization, the United Nations, was formed to replaced the failed League of Nations. The United Nations recognized Syria's statehood in 1946, and urged the French to leave the country. The last French troops left Syria that year on April 17, a date that is celebrated as Syria's national holiday.

Under the French mandate, economic conditions in Syria had grown worse during the Great Depression and World War II. Powerful families living in the cities owned most of the land, which was farmed by uneducated peasants. These peasants made up about two-thirds of the population. They had no access to services like education, sanitation, electricity, or paved roads. Farming methods had not changed in thousands of years. Tribal sheikhs held most of the local power in many areas.

At the same time, educated Syrians had become increasingly active in politics. Many ideas had begun to circulate as Syrians chafed under French rule. Some people wanted Greater Syria to be united under one independent government. Others believed that all Arabs had to unite for there to be a strong opposition against the Western governments that wanted to control them. They argued that Arab disunity and tribal loyalties had weakened Arabs in the eyes of Western nations. This argument was the foundation of the Pan-Arabism (*qawmiya*) movement. Opposing the Pan-Arabists were groups like the Muslim Brotherhood, who wanted a religious state ruled by Islamic law, similar to the way the Ottoman Empire had operated.

At the end of World War II, the Pan-Arabism movement produced official political parties in Syria, the most prominent of which was the Baath Party. *Baath* means "rebirth" in Arabic, and the Baath Party wanted a rebirth of Arab pride and the influence that Arab civilization had once enjoyed. It organized as a political party in 1947; today there are branches of the Baath Party in several Arab countries. In addition to aiming for Arab pride and unity, the Baath wanted to change the way society was organized. They supported socialism, a system in which the government, rather than private individuals, owns most of a country's industry. A socialist system— if working properly—excludes the possibility that a small group of people will own all of the country's wealth. Baath leaders felt the current system, which was managed by landowning nobility, was unfair, and they wanted to raise the standard of living of Syrian peasants.

Syria joined the Arab League in 1945. The other members were Egypt, Iraq, Lebanon, Saudi Arabia, Yemen, and Transjordan. More states joined as they achieved independence soon after the war. Transjordan became an independent state, renamed Jordan, in 1946. The Arab League wanted to present a united face to the outside world. The member states realized that because so many of their borders had been determined arbitrarily by foreign governments, territorial disputes could escalate into wars. They agreed that differences among the Arab states should be settled by negotiation, not by war.

Hundreds of years of Ottoman rule followed by French rule left the Syrians ill-prepared to create a stable government. Following World War II, as resistance against French rule became a common goal, Syrians experienced a rare moment of unity. Once they achieved that goal, however, their unity broke down. They struggled to find something to take the place of the foreign governments.

The first 20 years of Syria's independence were marked by a series of short-lived governments and political chaos. Most of Syria's leaders during this period rose through the military and seized power by force. Syria's first government, established during the French mandate, was dominated by the landowning nobility, who consisted of pro-hierarchical, anti-reformist Sunni Muslims. It had little support among the majority of Syrians.

THE POST-INDEPENDENCE YEARS

The issue of the Balfour Declaration and the Jewish national home-land was still hanging in the air after the end of World War II. Nazi Germany had tried to eliminate the Jewish people. When the world discovered the extent of the Nazis' cruelty, many people grew more sympathetic to the Zionist cause. They supported the idea of a Jewish state.

The year after Syria became independent, Great Britain announced that it would give up its mandate in Palestine. The United Nations developed a plan to divide the territory—the Palestine Partition Resolution. It stipulated that Palestine would be divided into two states, one Jewish and one Arab. The city of Jerusalem, which was important to both groups, would be placed under international control. The Jewish leadership in Palestine accepted the UN resolution. In May 1948 Jewish leaders announced the independence of the new Jewish state, Israel.

The Arab League rejected the Partition Resolution. Before the resolution was officially declared, Palestinian Arabs rushed to arms

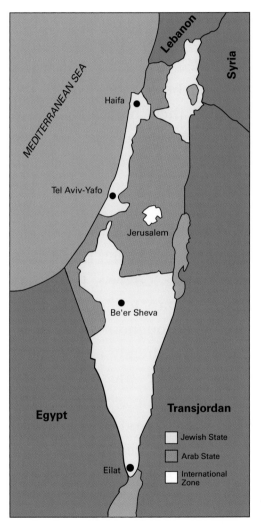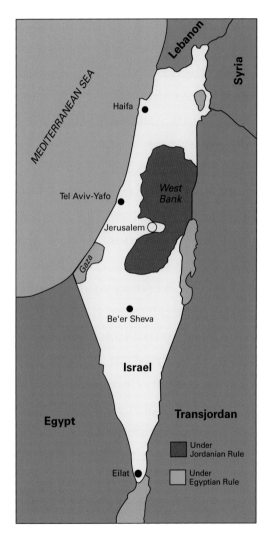

The map on the left shows the Jewish and Arab states that would have been created by the United Nations' 1947 partition plan for Palestine—a plan opposed by Syria and other Arab countries. When the British withdrew from Palestine in May 1948, the Arab forces attacked, determined to drive the Jews out of the country. The map on the right shows the boundaries of Israel at the end of the 1948–49 War of Independence.

to fight the Jewish state. The surrounding Arab countries quickly jumped to their aid. Many outraged Syrians still believed that Palestine was part of Greater Syria, and fought in Palestine along with Egyptians to secure the sections of land allotted to the Arabs. Jordan fought in Jerusalem for its own land interests.

When the 1948–49 war was over, the Egyptians occupied the Gaza Strip, and Jordan occupied the West Bank of the Jordan River and East Jerusalem. Syria occupied small strips of land around Lake Tiberias. However, Israel had expanded its control into areas that, according to the UN resolution, had been intended for the Palestinian Arabs. Many Palestinians fled their homes to live in refugee camps in other Arab countries, including Syria. A large number of Jews whose families had lived peacefully for centuries in Arab lands fled to Israel. These immigrants included many of the Jews who were living in Syria.

Since 1948, most Arabs have viewed Israel as a state arbitrarily created by Western governments. They have always felt that Israeli culture is Western and European, not Middle Eastern. Israel has also received a great deal of economic and military aid from Western countries, particularly the United States, throughout its history. Before the creation of Israel, the Arabs were already angry about European interference while they were under the rule of the Ottoman Empire and the mandates of the League of Nations. The Arab people's resentment of Israel thus goes hand in hand with their resentment of Western nations and their foreign policies.

In 1949, General Husni az-Zaim forced Syria's weak government out of office with backing from his troops. One coup followed another as Syria's military-controlled government continually changed hands. In 1954, a final coup ended the military governments, and the constitution was restored with an elected president and parliament. When parties were welcomed back into the political process, the Communist Party and the Baath Party were the best organized of the surviving parties. The Baath Party won a majority of the seats in Parliament.

The Baath Party believed the country's system of land ownership was holding back Syrian society. In 1958, in a move to break up the power of Syrian landowning families, the government limited the amount of land individuals could own. People with large landholdings were ordered to sell them within a certain time or the government would take the excess land. The government then loaned money to peasants and sold them land at very low prices. Additional land reform laws were passed in 1963 and 1980.

UNITED ARAB REPUBLIC AND THE BAATH PARTY

The president of Egypt, Gamal Abdel Nasser, was the strongest leader in the Arab world during the 1950s. Syria had been weak and unstable for several years. And so, with the Communist Party continually threatening to disrupt their political agenda, Baath leaders looked to Nasser and Egypt for assistance. They believed that uniting Syria with Egypt would provide the country with strong leadership and stability. Because Nasser was firmly against a multiple-party system, a union meant the end of the Baath Party. However, in reward for their loyalty to Nasser, Baath leaders envisioned special roles for themselves in the new state. Egypt felt that the union would stifle the threat of communism, and with Syria as an ally, it believed the two countries could more effectively fight their common enemy, Israel. The

Egyptian president Gamal Abdel Nasser encouraged the merger of Syria and Egypt as the United Arab Republic. This entity lasted only until 1961, when Syria withdrew.

Baath politicians passed a bill through the assembly to create the United Arab Republic.

The Syrians quickly grew unhappy with an Egyptian leadership that cared more about Egypt than Syria. Syria seceded from the United Arab Republic in 1961. The new government of Syria was conservative and dominated by notables, a social class of nobles with roots that reached as far back as the Ottoman Empire. Syrian government was more chaotic than ever after the breakup of the union with Egypt.

In March 1963 a small, secretive group of military officers overthrew the government. The group was dominated by members of Baath, many of whom were also members of religious minority groups. The military leaders of the alliance set up a civilian government with puppet leaders while pulling all the strings in the background. They continued to act secretly, and the public remained in the dark about who was in charge.

The Syrian political arena remained chaotic through the mid-1960s, with a rebellion erupting in Hama. The city was a center for the Sunni notable class and other religious conservatives, but the radical Muslim Brotherhood was also very active there. Conservatives feared the radical new government, and unrest grew in the city. The government put down the uprising in Hama with military force in 1964.

The fears of the notable class were realized on a larger scale when the Syrian government nationalized many private businesses in early 1965. Since then, the government has owned all businesses that distribute electricity and oil, process cotton, and conduct trade with other countries. The Baath Party was determined to break the power of the upper class and raise the conditions of the lower classes.

The 1960s saw the rise of two leaders, Salah al-Jadid and Hafiz al-Assad. These Baath Party members were also Alawis, who as a religious minority had been repressed and exploited until this point. But after successfully launching a coup in 1966, the two men helped further legitimize the Alawis in the eyes of Syrians. After the coup, Nureddin al-Atasi became prime minister, but Jadid remained the behind-the-scenes leader of Syria. Jadid had strong socialist leanings, and could not impose socialism on the country fast enough. People who came from the middle or notable class experienced discrimination in the military and the government. Meanwhile, members of the peasant class received preferential treatment and were promoted to higher ranks. Jadid established close ties with the Soviet government, which had already been providing military aid to Syria since the 1950s. It now offered economic aid as well.

THE SIX-DAY WAR AND ITS AFTERMATH

War broke out again with Israel in June 1967, after years of skirmishes between Syria and Israel near Lake Tiberias. The war, in which Israel fought the Syrian, Egyptian, and Jordanian armies, lasted only six days. It ended in complete success for Israel and disaster for the Arab states. Israel took the West Bank and East Jerusalem from Jordan, the Sinai Peninsula from Egypt, and the Golan Heights, including the town of Quneitra, from Syria.

That November, the United Nations Security Council adopted Resolution 242, which aimed at establishing a lasting peace in the Middle East. It called for Israeli withdrawal from territories it had gained in the Six-Day War, and that Arab states recognize Israel's right to exist as an independent nation. The resolution recognized the need to resolve the problem of the Palestinian refugees, although it offered no specific answers. After Resolution 242 was passed, the Israelis considered giving up territories, but at a summit in Khartoum, Sudan, the Arab states resolved against negotiations with Israel, and the two sides reached an impasse.

Most Arab states hoped to contain and control the Palestinian resistance. Israel, after all, was a powerful neighbor that gained more Arab territory in each successive conflict. Until 1967, the Arabs gave the Palestinians almost no voice in negotiations with Israel. After 1967, a group called the Palestinian Liberation Organization (PLO), led by Yasir Arafat, worked more closely toward attaining a Palestinian voice in the region's affairs.

The PLO was originally based in Gaza in 1964, with links to Cairo, Egypt. In 1968, the headquarters found another temporary location in Amman, Jordan. In September 1970, the Popular Front for the Liberation of Palestine hijacked three planes, two of which were brought down to Jordanian airstrips where the passengers were held hostage. Radical Palestinians wanted to bring down the Hashemite monarchy and use Jordan as a base to attack Israel. A civil war broke out that lasted several months. One year later, September 1971, the Jordanian army attacked remaining Palestinian militias. Hafiz al-Assad, by that time the Syrian Minister of Defense, sent an armored division into Jordan to back up the PLO, which Syria regarded as an ally against Israel. The Palestinians viewed Syria's attempt to help them as half-hearted and became angry. Meanwhile, the Jordanians felt completely alienated. They appealed to Israel and the United States for help against the Palestinians and the Syrians.

That same year, Assad took power from Jadid in a bloodless coup. Jadid controlled the Baath Party, but Assad completely controlled the military, and this had been a common route to power in Syria during the previous 25 years. Assad ordered the military to arrest Jadid and the key members of his government, and then quietly stepped into power. Jadid was imprisoned, and most of his supporters were exiled overseas. The military branch of the government was more moderate than the radical Baath Party. Immediately after the coup, Assad instituted changes to stabilize the government and shore up his power.

When national elections were held in 1971, the Baath Party nominated Assad for president, and the voters confirmed this choice in a national referendum. A referendum is an election in which the voters' only choice is whether to vote yes or no on a question, but in the case of an authoritarian government like Assad's, the legitimacy of the final vote is questionable. A 173-member legislature called the People's Council was also elected at this time. The Baath Party held a majority of the Council's seats.

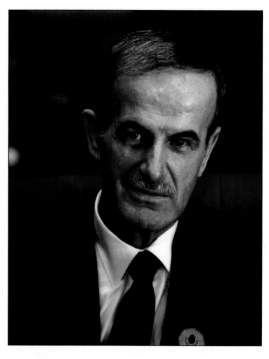

In November 1970 Hafiz al-Assad (1928–2000) led a coup that overthrew Salah Jadid; he became president of Syria in March 1971.

In 1973, a constitution was drafted. The new Baath government was too socialist and not religious enough for conservative Sunni Muslims, who wanted the constitution to make Islam the state religion. In order to pacify the Sunnis, the Baath changed the constitution. It required that the president of Syria be Muslim, although religious freedom was otherwise guaranteed.

In that same year, the Egyptians and Syrians attacked Israel in a joined effort to regain the territory they had lost in 1967. Though Syria could not recapture the Golan Heights, Israel did return Quneitra to Syria as part of the cease-fire agreement in 1974. Before pulling out of Quneitra, however, the Israelis inflicted a great deal of damage to the town, infuriating many Syrians.

Syria was less isolated from other countries under the Assad government than it had been in the past, but it continued to steer an independent course. Syria maintained close ties with the Soviet

Union, which provided military and economic assistance. This placed it in opposition to the United States.

Decades of constant political upheaval persuaded Assad to develop a more authoritarian regime. He won a firm grip on the government through control of the military, as well as independent security and intelligence units. These secret units kept a watchful eye on Syrian society and worked to prevent any political activity from taking place outside government channels. They arrested and imprisoned people they suspected of acts that were disloyal to the government.

CIVIL WAR IN LEBANON

After the PLO was banished from Jordan in 1971, Arafat moved the organization's headquarters to Lebanon. The PLO used the country as a base for attacks on Israel, which provoked Israel to retaliate. Although Lebanon had been a fairly stable country in the region, there were tensions between the Christians and Muslims who lived there. The Palestinian presence aggravated these tensions, and civil war broke out in 1975. After diplomatic negotiations failed to create peace, Syria sent troops into Lebanon.

In June 1982, Israel invaded Lebanon to support the Christian Maronites contending with the PLO. The Israelis hoped that through their support of the Maronites they could find an Arab Christian ally to fight against the Arab Muslims of the region. Israel soon occupied Lebanon, and its intervention eventually gave rise to Hezbollah, a radical Shiite Muslim group that opposed the Israeli presence there. Hezbollah used kidnappings and other terrorist tactics to further its agenda against Israel and the West.

The United Nations sent peacekeeping forces to Lebanon in 1983. A terrorist bomb killed 50 people at the American *embassy* in April. Another 260 U.S. Marines and 60 French soldiers died when truck bombs were detonated near their barracks later in the year. The peacekeeping countries withdrew in 1984, and a year later Israeli troops withdrew to southern Lebanon, near the Israeli border. There they continued to occupy a "security zone," from which they fought Hezbollah and tried to prevent terrorist attacks on Israeli territory. Approximately 30,000 Syrian troops remained stationed in Lebanon as well.

Assad continued to endorse the Baath opinion that Arabs are stronger working together than they are working separately. As a result, he consistently opposed negotiations and treaties between Israel and individual Arab states. He wanted the Arab states to negotiate from a position of unity and strength. He also insisted that Israel had to uphold its end of Resolution 242 and withdraw to its old borders before the Arabs would agree to a lasting peace. The Syrian leadership believed the Arab world suffered a blow in 1979 when Anwar el-Sadat, the president of Egypt, signed a separate peace treaty with Israel. Egypt recognized Israel and established *diplomatic relations* with it in exchange for Israel's return of the Sinai Peninsula to Egypt.

The Western world hailed the treaty, which was mediated by the United States, as a giant step toward establishing peace in the Middle East. But many Arabs were enraged, feeling their strongest ally had betrayed them. They ejected Egypt from the Arab League and moved the League's headquarters from Cairo, Egypt, to Tunis, Tunisia. Egypt's membership in the Arab League would not be restored until 1989, when League headquarters were moved back to Cairo. In 1981 Sadat was assassinated by extremists who were opposed to Egypt's peaceful negotiations with Israel.

The 1980s was a difficult decade for Syria. Several years of drought debilitated its agriculture, and the troops stationed in Lebanon were a drain on the Syrian economy. Syria sided with Iran against Iraq when war erupted between the two countries in 1980, but it did not fight in the conflict. The decision to support Iran over

The remains of a U.S. Marine barracks in Beirut, Lebanon. The building was destroyed in an explosion in October 1983, and 241 Marines were killed. U.S. troops had been deployed in Beirut as part of a multinational peacekeeping force in the summer of 1982; their mission was to try to stabilize war-torn Lebanon. After similar attacks on the barracks for French and Italian troops, the peacekeeping mission ended in failure the next year.

another Arab state isolated Syria from its allies. In addition to all of these problems, unrest in the country prompted the government to take harsh measures against its own people.

The Muslim Brotherhood continued to oppose Baath Party rule and to clamor for the establishment of a conservative Sunni Muslim state. In 1979, the Muslim Brotherhood initiated a series of attacks targeting Baath Party officials and members of the military. In response to these attacks, the government cracked down harshly on the Muslim opposition. Membership in the Muslim Brotherhood became a crime punishable by death. In 1982, an elite military unit led by Assad's brother Rifaat attacked and bombed the city of Hama, rooting out cells of the Muslim Brotherhood that were sheltered there. Although the exact figures are not known, it is believed that at least 25,000 people died in the attacks.

During the 1980s, Syria angered Western nations by supporting the activities of Hezbollah and other terrorist organizations in Lebanon. Syria was known to supply these organizations with weapons, funding, and military training. In addition, several terrorist attacks overseas were traced back to Syria, including an attempt to plant a bomb aboard an Israeli jetliner traveling from London to Tel Aviv.

After more than 10 years of continuous fighting in Lebanon, the Lebanese parliament, aided by Syria and other Arab countries, created an agreement for peace and strong civil government at a 1989 meeting in Saudi Arabia. The agreement, called the Taif Accord, outlined plans for a government in which power would be shared more fairly between Christians and Muslims. It called for the complete withdrawal of Israeli troops from southern Lebanon. The agreement also stated that Syrian troops would withdraw from Beirut and retreat to Lebanon's Bekaa Valley once Israeli troops were gone, and that Syrian troops would completely withdraw from Lebanon in two years. Also, Syria and Lebanon would decide together whether to continue using Syrian troops in Lebanon. However, neither Israel nor Syria withdrew their soldiers from Lebanon during the 1990s.

The Syrian economy improved in the 1990s thanks to increased oil prices and good harvests. The government also made slight changes to relax government control of the economy. To sustain its economy, however, Syria continued to rely heavily on foreign aid from countries of the Persian Gulf, as well as those of the West. For years, Syria owed billions of dollars to the Soviet Union.

THE PERSIAN GULF WAR

Iraqi president Saddam Hussein invaded the tiny Arab country of Kuwait in 1990. He soon annexed Kuwait, claiming it as part of Iraq. King Fahd of Saudi Arabia, who feared his own country might be Iraq's next target, asked for international support against Saddam Hussein. When diplomacy failed, a coalition of 34 countries, led by the United States, went to war with Iraq. Although some states of the Arab League chose not to go to war against another Arab country, Syria and many other Arab countries joined the coalition that fought against Iraq.

After the Persian Gulf War, Syria's relations with the international community improved slightly. When leaders of the United States and Soviet Union invited Middle Eastern countries to a peace conference in Madrid during 1991, Syria attended. At this conference, the Arab countries expressed a willingness to make peace, acknowledge Israel's right to exist, and establish diplomatic relations. In return for peace, they insisted that Israel turn Palestinian-occupied territory over to the Palestinians so they could establish their own state. They also demanded that Palestinian refugees living in other countries be allowed to return to their former homeland.

Throughout the 1990s, Syria participated in peace negotiations with Israel several times, but there were few advances. The Syrian government continued to insist there would be no peace until all Arab peoples, including the Palestinians, were at peace with Israel. In 1994, Jordan disrupted Syria's agenda by becoming the second Arab country to sign a peace treaty with Israel.

Israel has claimed a willingness to return the Golan Heights in exchange for peace and normal relations with Syria, but the two sides cannot agree on their borders. Syria insists on restoring the line defined in the 1949 armistice. Israel prefers the border that was established by the League of Nations mandate for Palestine in

1923. The difference is only a few miles, but the 1949 armistice line gives Syria access to Lake Tiberias, a valuable water resource, and the 1923 international border does not.

The Israelis and the Palestinians also began negotiating ways to live together peacefully during the 1990s. With the Oslo Accords, signed in Norway in 1993, each side recognized the other's political and civil rights in Palestine. Israel also recognized the Palestinian Authority, made up of PLO leaders, as representative of the Palestinian people and agreed to negotiate with Yasir Arafat. In return, Arafat renounced the use of "terrorism and other acts of violence," which until the Oslo Accords had been the most common fighting tactic of the Palestinians. Israel agreed to allow the Palestinians' limited self-rule in the West Bank and the Gaza Strip as well. To carry out their self-rule, the Palestinians elected Yasir Arafat as president of the Palestinian National Authority in 1996.

Although the PLO had renounced terrorism, several other terrorist organizations remained active in Israel, including Hezbollah and Hamas. The Israeli people were sharply divided in their opinions about peace with the Palestinians. As a result, they elected several different leaders during this time, all with different attitudes toward peace. Negotiations broke down, and violence erupted again between Israel and the Palestinians in 2000. Peace negotiations between Syria and Israel also stalled during that year, as neither side would give up any of its demands. In 2001, the Arab League asked its members to break off all relations and all negotiations with Israel as long as it continued to use violence to deal with the Palestinians.

In May of 2000, Israel finally pulled its troops out of southern Lebanon. One year later, Syria withdrew most of its troops stationed in Beirut and relocated them elsewhere in Lebanon, in accordance with the first step outlined in the Taif Accord. The Syrian troops were moved to the Bekaa Valley near the Syrian border the following April, but they remained in Lebanon past the Taif deadline for complete withdrawal.

TRANSFER OF PRESIDENTIAL POWER

Syrian president Hafiz al-Assad died in June 2000 after 30 years as Syria's leader. The relative stability in Syria under Assad's leadership had been based on his authoritarian rule and swift reaction to any dissent. Many wondered if the Syrian government would sink into chaos after his death. The government and the Baath Party moved quickly to ensure that there would be no major changes.

Hafiz al-Assad had been preparing his son Bashar to become president since 1994. On the day Assad died, government leaders loyal to him named Bashar commander-in-chief of the armed forces. Firm control of the military would eliminate the possibility of a military coup. Bashar al-Assad took his father's place as Secretary-General of the Baath Party the same day. The Syrian constitution required that the president be at least 40 years old, and Bashar was only 34. The constitution was quickly changed, and the Baath Party nominated Bashar al-Assad for president. He was elected in a national referendum that July. (No other candidate was allowed to participate in the election.)

At first, Syrians believed Bashar would be more politically liberal than his father. The new president spoke occasionally about implementing government reforms, and permitted some modest freedoms during 2000 and 2001. Ultimately, however, there were no major changes in Syrian politics during the 2010s. The Emergency Law, which gave the government broad authority to arrest anyone considered a threat to the regime, remained in force. Syria's government released some political prisoners in 2001, but over the next decade hundreds of other dissidents were arrested and imprisoned when they spoke out against the government. To date, the Syrian reforms have mainly been economic, including the establishment of a stock market and privatization of banks.

The 2003 U.S. invasion of Iraq created problems for Syria. The conflict in Iraq displaced thousands of people, who began to cross the border into cities likes Aleppo and Damascus in an attempt to escape the violence and destruction. In 2004 the U.S. government imposed additional sanctions on Syria because of its support for terrorist groups like Hamas and Hezbollah, as well as its willingness to allow foreign militants to cross its borders into Iraq, where they waged an insurgency against the occupying American troops that were attempting to rebuild the country.

In February 2005, former Lebanese prime minister Rafic Hariri was killed by a bomb in Beirut. Hariri had been strongly opposed to the continued Syrian military presence in Lebanon. An investigation by the United Nations determined that the Syrian government had been involved in the assassination. Angered at the Syrian role, large-scale public demonstrations occurred throughout Lebanon until Syria removed its troops in April 2005.

Between 2008 and 2010, Syria's relationship with the United States improved. The country resumed peace talks with Israel, and

Former United Nations secretary-general Kofi Annan (left) acted as an envoy for the U.N. and the Arab League when he visited Damascus in 2012 to discuss Syria's response to rebel forces and propose a plan for peace to Bashar al-Assad.

a special envoy from the United States visited Damascus to work with the Syrians on Middle East peace. In 2010 the United States re-established diplomatic relations with Syria, sending an ambassador to Damascus and lifting some sanctions. However, the thaw in relations soon ended. In May 2010 the United States once again broke off relations, accusing the Syrian government of illegally providing missiles to Hezbollah in Lebanon and of pursuing chemical and nuclear weapons.

CIVIL WAR IN SYRIA

In late 2010 and early 2011, anti-government protests began to occur in a number of Arab countries. The protests—which became known as the Arab Spring—were aimed at improving the political circumstances and living conditions of the Arab people. In Syria, the first sign of the Arab Spring was the appearance of anti-regime graffiti in the city of Daraa. The Syrian government responded by arresting the students who were responsible. This led to larger protests. Inspired by successful revolutions in Tunisia and Egypt, Syrian protesters used marches, hunger strikes, rioting, vandalism, and guerrilla attacks to destabilize the Assad regime. The Syrian police and military used force in an effort to quell the demonstrations, but despite the deaths of several people the unrest soon spread throughout the country.

By August 2011, the protests had turned into a violent uprising, with the United Nations and many countries condemning the Syrian government's use of heavy weaponry against rebel forces, as well as the killing of civilians. Several countries, including the United States and Turkey, began to arm and train rebel groups, while militant Islamist groups in places like Iraq and Libya began to send fighters to Syria.

In June 2012, the Free Syrian Army gained control over most of Aleppo, as well as several other cities and towns in Syria. That rebel group was formed of former Syrian Army officers and soldiers, and trained and supplied by Turkey and the U.S. In November, representatives of the Free Syrian Army met with leaders of other rebel groups in Qatar, where they agreed to form the National Coalition for Syrian Revolutionary and Opposition Forces. (For the most part, Islamist groups fighting in Syria refused to join the Coalition, however.)

The United States, Turkey, Great Britain, France, and more than 120 other countries soon granted official recognition to the National Coalition as the legitimate representative of the Syrian people. This added another element of international pressure to the regime, which was already dealing with economic sanctions imposed by the Arab League, the European Union, Turkey, and the United States. Beginning in 2012, the United Nations and Arab League sent sev-

The wreckage of government tanks blocks the street in front of a badly damaged mosque in Aleppo. Rebel forces captured the city in 2012.

A pair of U.S. Air Force F-15E Strike Eagles fly over northern Iraq after conducting airstrikes against ISIL targets in Syria, September 2014.

eral special envoys to meet with government leaders in the region and try to resolve the Syrian crisis.

The year 2013 saw the rise of the Islamic State of Iraq and the Levant (ISIL), which was able to capture and hold territory in both Iraq and Syria. That same year, the Assad government was accused of introducing chemical weapons into the civil war. This led to renewed demands for Bashar al-Assad to relinquish power, as well as a threat by U.S. President Barack Obama to consider military options within Syria to remove the Assad regime. Under international pressure, the Syrian government agreed to destroy its chemical weapons through a U.N.-supervised process.

During 2014, the United Nations began holding peace negotiations between the Assad regime and rebel groups. However, the talks went nowhere as Bashar al-Assad refused to step down and turn over power to a transitional government. The Syrian military instead used the cease-fire to prepare for new offensives against rebel positions in Aleppo and elsewhere.

In June 2014, soon after conquering the city of Mosul in neighboring Iraq, ISIL declared itself a caliphate that ruled the territory it controlled. As reports of ISIL atrocities committed against

Christians, Kurds, and Shiite Muslims were reported, the United States and other countries agreed to intervene with military force. Airstrikes were launched against ISIL positions, although the U.S. and other countries decided not to send in soldiers to wage ground combat.

By 2015, according to the United Nations, more than 220,000 people had been killed in the Syrian civil war, while more than 9 million Syrians—roughly half of the population—were refugees. Syrian civilians have suffered greatly during the war. A UN study found that both sides had engaged in acts that would be considered war crimes—rape, murder, and torture. The Assad regime has used "barrel bombs"—improvised explosive devices dropped from aircraft —to devastate both civilian and rebel populations and turn Syria's once-proud cities into rubble. Tragically, it appears this conflict will not end any time soon.

 Text-Dependent Questions

1. In what year did Syria gain independence?
2. What is the Baath Party?
3. How did Hafez al-Assad react when Muslim Brotherhood protests against his government occurred in the city of Hama in 1982?
4. What event prompted Syria to withdraw its troops from Lebanon in 2005?
5. What organization has been recognized by more than 130 nation-states as the official representative of the Syrian people?

 Research Project

Decisions made at the Paris Peace Conference of 1919, which was held after World War I, helped to reshape the modern world by creating new countries from the colonies or territories of the conquered powers (Germany, the Austro-Hungarian Empire, and the Ottoman Empire.) These new countries did not immediately gain independence; existing nations like France and Britain were given authority (known as a mandate) to rule them until they were ready for full independence. Using the Internet or your school library, find out more about the League of Nations and the mandate system, and write a two-page report on it. Was the mandate system a success, or a failure? Provide real-world examples to support your position.

The Umayyad Mosque, also known as the Grand Mosque of Damascus, was built after Muslim forces captured the city in the seventh century. It was constructed on the site of a Christian basilica dedicated to John the Baptist, who is honored as a prophet by both Christians and Muslims. Construction of the mosque was completed in 715 CE.

The Economy, Politics, and Religion

Syria has a socialist economy. The government owns and controls many industries and sets prices for essential items, especially staple foods like grain. All Syrian banks are government owned. Every five years, the president draws up an economic plan dictating economic goals and priorities for the next five years. In controlling the economy, the government has tried to equalize the incomes and opportunities available to people from different social classes and in different areas of the country.

The government has made recent attempts to stimulate economic growth. In 2004, four private banks began to operate, and the idea of creating stock market was discussed. The idea eventually became a plan, and in 2009 a Damascus Stock Exchange opened. Many people considered these moves to be steps in a positive direction toward solving the economic problems of Syria. However, in the past five years the civil war has completely thrown all plans for economic development in Syria off track.

The government owns utilities like electrical power generation, telephone lines, and water distribution. The government also owns the railroads, trucks, and buses that move products from one area of the country to another. Heavy industry, which includes oil drilling and mining, is also government owned. Private individuals and businesses are allowed to own farms and factories, as well as shops and other small businesses. The government also allows joint public and private ownership of certain types of businesses in order to encourage the investment of private money without the complete loss of government control. The government owns about 25 percent of these joint-venture firms.

Only one in four Syrians participates in the workforce. Of those people who are employed, quite a few are forced to have more than one job to supplement their incomes. One reason for this low level of employment is the Syrian population's uneven distribution. Almost half of all Syrians are school-age children. The employment levels of Syrian women are especially low. In the cities, only one woman out of every ten engages in paid employment.

Nineteen percent of Syria's 5.5 million workers earn their living in agriculture, 15 percent work in industry, and 66 percent work

Words to Understand in This Chapter

exports—goods that are sold to other countries.

hajj—a pilgrimage to Mecca required of all Muslims.

Qur'an—the book containing the sacred writings of the Muslims, which they believe is the word of Allah dictated to Muhammad by the angel Gabriel.

Ramadan—the ninth month of the Islamic calendar, when Muslims fast and pray to commemorate the appearance of the angel Gabriel to the prophet Muhammad.

Sunna—Muslim traditions based on the words and actions of Muhammad.

The flag of Syria, which was adopted in 1982, is very similar to the
flags of several of its neighbors.
Iraq's flag follows the same design
but adds a third star and an Arabic
inscription. Egypt's flag includes
the red, white, and black horizontal
stripes, but instead of the stars a
heraldic eagle is centered on the
flag.

in service industries. Those in the service industries include doc-
tors, teachers, bus drivers, and maids. The unemployment rate—
the percentage of people who are available to work but don't have
jobs—is about 20 percent. Many Syrians have avoided unemployment by working overseas, particularly in the Gulf Arab states. The
money they send home to their families is a much-needed boost to
the economy, but Syria still needs a better-educated workforce in
order to compete in the modern global economy.

Every year, Syria receives more than $100 million in foreign aid,
most of which comes from the oil-producing Gulf states. The
European Union and Japan have also provided economic assistance to Syria in the past, although such aid ended when the civil
war began.

MODERNIZATION

Oil is Syria's most lucrative industry. Oil and petroleum products
account for the bulk of Syria's export revenue. Unfortunately, Syria
appears to lack the vast oil reserves that bless many other Arab
states. Despite Syria's poverty, high unemployment, and economic
problems, modern development has improved the country's standard

Colorful carpets hang in a market in Damascus. The textile industry has traditionally employed many Syrians.

of living a great deal since World War II.

By 1992, 95 percent of Syria's villages had electricity. Most areas of the country also have water pipes and a safe supply of clean drinking water. Some areas, however, still rely on water that is shipped in on trucks. With 3.5 million telephone lines in use in 2014, telephones have become more common to Syria, but there are some households in rural areas that still do not own them.

Many roads have been laid to open up rural areas. In 2014, about 25 percent of Syria's roads were paved. Syria's mountains have been a serious obstacle to **exports** in the past because they cut off the interior of the country from the coast, where goods can be shipped overseas. A railroad that travels across the mountains between the agricultural region of the Ghab and the port of Latakia has allowed faster, more efficient transportation of products to the coast. The civil war has had a devastating effect on Syria's infrastructure.

AGRICULTURE AND INDUSTRY

Syria has been forced to find better ways to feed its growing population. For this reason, the government has focused heavily on agriculture in its economic planning. Syria faces several environmental problems that impact the land's ability to feed its people. Only 20

Quick Facts: The Economy of Syria

Gross domestic product (GDP*): $107.6 billion (rank 73rd in the world)
GDP per capita: $5,100 (rank 159th in the world)
GDP growth rate: −2.3% (rank 213nd in the world)
Inflation: 59.1% (2013 est.) (rank 223rd in the world)
Unemployment Rate: 17.8% (2013 est.) (rank 155th in the world)
Natural resources: petroleum, natural gas, phosphates, sulfur
Agriculture (18% of GDP): wheat, barley, cotton, lentils, chickpeas, olives, sugar beets; beef, mutton, eggs, poultry, milk (2013 est.)
Industry (22% of GDP): petroleum, textiles, food processing, beverages, tobacco, phosphate rock mining, cement, oil seeds crushing, automobile assembly (2013 est.)
Services (60% of GDP): government, banking, other (2013 est.)
Foreign trade:
   Imports—$8.917 billion: machinery and transport equipment, electric power machinery, food and livestock, metal and metal products, chemicals and chemical products, plastics, yarn, paper (2013 est.)
   Exports—$2.675 billion: crude oil, minerals, petroleum products, fruits and vegetables, cotton fiber, textiles, clothing, meat and live animals, wheat (2013 est.)
Currency exchange rate: 189 Syrian pounds = U.S. $1 (2015)

*GDP, or gross domestic product, is the total value of goods and services produced in a country annually. All figures are 2011 estimates unless otherwise noted. The war-driven deterioration of the economy has resulted in a disappearance of quality national level statistics since then.
Source: CIA World Factbook, 2015.

percent of Syria's farmland is watered by irrigation. The rest is dependent on unreliable rains and is frequently hit by droughts. In addition, too many wells have depleted the ground water, and many of the rivers are becoming polluted. Syria's soil also needs serious attention. Topsoil erosion, plus the repeated growth of the same crops on the same fields without the addition of fertilizer, has exhausted the soil in many areas. Fertilizers and crop rotation are necessary to improve the soil's nutrient content so healthy crops can grow.

Syrians have been making and exporting textiles for hundreds of years. Cotton is one of Syria's principal crops. Cotton cloth and cotton clothing are manufactured in Syria. Silk weaving and leather tanning are also important industries. In addition to textiles, Syrian factories produce soap, cement, glass, matches, bottled beverages, fertilizer, processed foods, and household appliances.

Over time the private business sector has been gradually expanding. Shops have always been privately owned. Merchants and artisans often work in family-owned businesses. Many Syrian products are still made by hand in small artisans' workshops, just as they have been for centuries.

POLITICS

In hopes of quelling public protests during the civil war, the Assad regime drafted a new constitution, which would set the framework for the state's government. It was ratified in a national referendum, and became effective on February 27, 2012. This document superseded an earlier constitution written in 1973.

A major change in the new constitution was that it weakened the Baath Party, which previously had been the dominant party in government and Syrian society. The 1973 constitution had been designed to ensure that the Baath Party would remain in power. The 2012 constitution also provides for national, multi-party elections—something that was not permitted previously. Under the 1973 constitution, the Baath Party nominated one candidate to the presidency. The Syrian people then voted whether or not to approve the party's nominee. The people always voted "yes"—in 2007, for example, Bashar al-Assad received 98 percent of the vote.

Under the 2012 constitution, a presidential election was held in June 2014 with two candidates challenging Assad for the presidency. Despite the pretense of democracy, most international observers considered the election to be a sham, as Assad received 88 percent of the vote. Many people who opposed the Assad regime refused to participate in the election, and the chaos of the civil war made it impossible for refugees and others to cast ballots.

Despite the constitutional changes, the president of Syria continues to have great power. The president controls almost all government appointments, foreign relations, the armed services, and the economy. He has the power to declare war, draft all the country's laws, and make changes to the constitution.

Syrians elect representatives to the 250-member People's Council for four-year terms. After the most recent election in 2012, 168 of the seats were held by members of the National Progressive Front, a coalition of political parties dominated by the Baath Party and supportive of the Assad regime. There are more than 70 seats held by representatives who are not affiliated with a political party; again, most of them are Assad supporters. The Popular Front for Change and Liberation, an anti-Assad coalition, has five seats in the People's Council. The People's Council approves or vetoes laws proposed by the president.

The Syrian legal system is a mixture of Islamic, French, and Ottoman law. There are separate religious, civil, and criminal courts. The president appoints judges in the Syrian courts to four-year terms. There are also military courts that operate apart from the judicial system.

Two and a half years of military service is mandatory for all men over 19. The Syrian military includes 400,000 active-duty and reserve troops. The president handpicks the members of elite military units. Because they depend on the president for their position, they tend to be loyal to him. Only these troops are allowed to be stationed in Damascus. This law is designed to prevent a military coup of the presidency.

The president also maintains security and intelligence agencies that operate independently of one another and answer only to him. These secretive agencies monitor every aspect of Syrian life. Agents often disguise themselves as people working in the general population. The agencies are an important key to the president's tight control over the country, and further ensure that he will stay in power.

Syrian citizens basically have no real civil rights. They have no freedom of speech, and everything they say may be overheard by intelligence agents or secret police. Gatherings for anything but religious worship are very closely monitored and treated with suspicion. The government fears grassroots political organizations that might try to undermine its power. The constitution grants Syrians certain rights, though in practice the government has withheld many of those rights.

RELIGION

The Syrian constitution provides for freedom of religion, and for the most part, the government respects it in practice. The constitution does, however, require the president of Syria to be a Muslim, and also establishes that Syrian Muslims should be governed by Islamic religious law, known as Sharia, in addition to the civil and criminal legal codes. The Islamic legal courts collectively make up one branch of the Syrian judicial system.

Almost all Syrians are monotheists, people who believe in only one God. The majority of Syrians are Sunni Muslims. Sixteen percent of Syrians belong to minority Muslim sects, and about 10 percent are Christians. Although Syria used to have a sizable Jewish population, most Jews have emigrated in response to the tension between Syria and Israel.

The Islamic faith dominates Syrian culture and daily life as it does in most Islamic countries. *Islam* means "submission" in Arabic. Muslims are supposed to submit themselves to God (*Allah* in Arabic) and follow the teachings of Muhammad, whose sayings are recorded in the Muslim holy book, the **Qur'an** (or Koran). Islam teaches that the Qur'an is the word of God revealed to Muhammad by the angel Gabriel. In addition to the Qur'an, Muslims follow the **Sunna**, a collection of sayings and teachings of the Prophet. Together, the Qur'an and the *Sunna* make up *Sharia*, which for hundreds of years was the only form of law in several Muslim countries.

Muslims believe the words of the Jewish prophets of the biblical Old Testament. They also believe that Jesus Christ, the founder of Christianity, was a prophet sent by God. They consider Jews and Christians fellow "people of the Book." But for Muslims, Muhammad was the final prophet sent by God to correct and clarify errors made by the earlier prophets. He was the last prophet God sent because his life and testaments are the final and perfect truth.

The five pillars of Islam are actions that every faithful Muslim is supposed to perform. The first is to believe and faithfully recite the *Shahada*, the declaration of the faith, which consists of these words: "There is no god but Allah, and Muhammad is His Prophet." The second pillar is prayer. There are two types of prayer in Islam, *Salat* and *Du'a*. *Salat* is a set of prayers that Muslims must say five times each day while they face Mecca. These prayers consist of the *Shahada* and passages from the Qur'an. *Salat* is performed at sunrise, midday, afternoon, sunset, and evening. The second form of

Did You Know?

Muhammad and his followers fled Mecca and moved to Medina in CE 622. This journey is known as the Hijrah. For Muslims, 622 is the first year of the Islamic era, which is marked by the Hijrah. Because Islam follows a lunar calendar, the Muslim year is only about 354 days, unlike the solar year of 365 days. Years since the Hijrah are designated with the initials AH, which stands for *anno hegirae*, (Latin for "year of the Hijrah"). The initials AH are used in a similar fashion to the initials BCE and CE, or the older BC and AD.

prayer, *Du'a*, is unstructured personal prayer, and is not required.

The third pillar is the **hajj**. All Muslims are required, if capable, to make a pilgrimage to Mecca at least once in their lifetimes. The hajj takes place every year between the seventh and tenth days of the last month in the Muslim calendar. Pilgrims take part in a festival at the Mosque of Mecca during the hajj. Although it is not required, many pilgrims also travel to Medina to pray at Muhammad's grave. The fourth pillar is *Sawm*, a required fast during the month of **Ramadan**, the ninth month of the Islamic calendar. The fifth pillar is *Zakat* (charity), which requires Muslims to give money to the needy.

The Muslim place of worship is called a mosque. The wall of the prayer hall that faces toward Mecca is marked by a special niche indicating the direction worshippers should face during prayer. It is common in Muslim countries to hear men called *muezzins* announce the next prayer time from the tops of minarets, or tall towers.

The Muslim day of prayer is Friday. It is a day off from work and school in Islamic countries, and many people worship at a mosque on that day. Prayers in the mosque are generally led by a prayer leader called an *imam*.

Islamic teachings forbid using force to convert non-believers. Muslims have to choose to believe. When Muslims conquered new lands, monotheists were allowed to continue practicing their own religions freely, although they had the option of converting to Islam, which had social and legal advantages. Those who weren't "people of the book" had three choices: they could convert, become slaves, or die. Technically, however, they were not forced to choose Islam.

Although Muslims are not supposed to use force in converting others, traditional Islamic law does impose on them a religious obligation to spread the Islamic faith throughout the world. This has been interpreted to mean that all the people of the world should become either Muslims or subjects of Muslim rulers. This concept of spreading Islamic law is known as jihad. It is usually interpreted as waging a holy war. Muhammad and his followers were fighting the jihad when they conquered the Middle East. Those who die fighting the jihad are considered martyrs for the faith. The Qur'an states that those who fight the jihad will be rewarded on earth and in heaven.

MUSLIM SECTS

All Muslims follow the Qur'an and *Sharia*. Because these two texts guide all Islamic sects, the differences among the sects are generally more root-

A page from the Qur'an, the holy book of Islam. Syrian law is based on Islamic laws outlined in the Qur'an, the *Sunna*, and the *Hadith*, a collection of stories about the prophet Muhammad.

The mosque in Sayyidah Zaynab, a village near Damascus, is believed to be the burial place of Muhammad's granddaughter. Her tomb is a pilgrimage site for Syrian Shiites.

ed in society and politics than religious beliefs. Early in the history of Islam, a disagreement developed over the religious leadership of the Muslim community. Sunni Muslims believed that the leader of Islam should be elected. Shiites believed that the position should be inherited through the line of Ali, Muhammad's cousin.

Sunni means "orthodox path" and refers to people who follow the *Sunna*. Most of the Muslims throughout the world are Sunnis. Shiites form the majority in only four Arab countries: Lebanon, Bahrain, Iran, and Iraq. They often tend to be more radical in their religious practices than Sunni Muslims, although the Muslim Brotherhood, a Sunni sect, is just as radical in practice as many Shiite sects. The majority of Shiites are members of the lower social classes, living in rural areas. Most strongly believe in martyrdom, and the theme of persecution runs through the general Shiite interpretation of Islamic history. They are more flexible with Islamic doctrine, stressing that it can be modified and expanded on. Some Shiites have broken off into additional sects, such as the Imami Shiites (also knows as the Twelver Shiites) and the Ismailis.

Some Shiite sects have adopted a policy of extreme secrecy. As a result, their exact beliefs are not well known or understood. Believers can only be born into these groups, which do not accept converts. They guard their beliefs carefully for fear of being persecuted as heretics by the Sunni majority. Several of these sects form sizable minorities in areas of Syria.

The Alawis form the largest Muslim minority group in Syria. They have traditionally lived in western Syria in the Nusayriyah Mountains near Latakia and have had little contact with outsiders. The Alawis' situation is changing, however, as they have risen to power in Syria through the military, the government, and the Baath Party. Today more of them live in Damascus, attend school, and mix with the general population. Most Alawis believe that Muhammad, Ali, and Salman, a friend and companion of Muhammad, are divine. For this reason, Sunnis consider Alawis heretics, accusing them of denying that there is only one God. Alawi clerics claim that the Alawis are a sect of Shiite Muslims who faithfully follow the teachings of the Qur'an.

The Ismailis are a small group of Imami Shiites. In the past, they have tended to be religious extremists and political revolutionaries. Their beliefs are shrouded in secrecy. A small number of Ismailis live in villages in the western mountains

 Did You Know?

President Bashar al-Assad is a member of the Alawi religious minority. Although they form a small percentage of the Syrian population, Alawis and other minorities dominate the military and hold many prominent government and Baath Party positions.

Although most Syrians are Muslims, the country does have a larger Christian population than most other Arab countries. About 10 percent of Syrians are Christian. This village, called Ma'loula, is one of very few places where the inhabitants still speak Aramaic, the language spoken at the time of Jesus. Christians and Muslims both live in the village, which has been the scene of several battles during the civil war.

of Syria. The Druze are an offshoot sect of the Ismailis, with doctrines so unconventional that much of Islam does not consider them to be really Muslim. The Druze live in Damascus, Aleppo, and around the Jebel Arab range.

The Yazidis are a very small Kurdish-speaking minority concentrated in a few villages northwest of Aleppo. Little is known about their beliefs other than that they honor the Bible and the Qur'an.

Most of Syria's Christians live in cities. Before the Muslim conquest, almost all Syrians were Christians. Although most converted to Islam, a number of them did not. Today, Syrian

Christians belong to a number of different Christian churches. These include the Syrian Orthodox Church, the Armenian Orthodox Church, the Greek Orthodox Church, the Greek Catholic Church, and the Syrian Catholic Church. Christian liturgies (rites of worship) are conducted in a number of different languages: Arabic, Greek, Armenian, Aramaic, and Syriac.

 ## Text-Dependent Questions

1. What environmental problems do farmers in Syria face?
2. What is the largest Muslim minority group in Syria? How do their beliefs differ from other Muslim sects?
3. What does the Arabic word *Sunna* mean?

 ## Research Project

The division of Islam into Sunni and Shia branches dates back to the seventh century. Using your school library or the Internet, find out more about Ali, Muhammad's son-in-law and companion who became the fourth caliph in 656 ce. Write a two-page report about Ali, and how his assassination in 661 led to the Sunni-Shia split. Include some examples of how these two Muslim sects have clashed throughout history, to the present day.

A Syrian boy holds his sister in a Red Crescent refugee camp on the border with Turkey. Syria's population is believed to be around 18 million, but many of these people have been forced to flee their homes due to the civil war.

The People

The bulk of the Syria's population today has its origins in the Semitic tribes that populated the area in ancient times, but their culture is greatly influenced by the Arabs who invaded this region during the seventh century. Many Syrians are of Arab descent, and Arabic is the predominant language in the country. Syrian society is shaped by the core values of religion and family.

Today the country of Syria has has a population of nearly 18 million. This figure is misleading, as the U.N. High Commissioner for Refugees (UNHCR) noted that by 2015 more than 2.25 million Syrians had fled their homes due to the ongoing civil war, and were living in refugee camps in neighboring Lebanon, Jordan, or Turkey. Another 7.5 million are listed as "internally displaced," meaning they've been forced to leave their homes and live elsewhere within the country.

The civil war has disrupted all aspects of society in Syria. Accurate **demographic data** is difficult to find due to violence and unrest, and many Syrians have had to make changes to their lifestyles due to the conflict. Nonetheless, this chapter will attempt to discuss the traditional way of life, as well as how the civil war has affected Syria.

FAMILY

For many centuries, families in the Syria region were organized into clans and tribes. Many Syrians, particularly Bedouins, Kurds, Alawis, and Druze, still consider themselves loyal members of a tribe, rather than loyal to the Syrian state. In Syria, nearly all other ties—friendship, work relationships, political connections—come second to family and to confessional (religious) affiliation. To a Syrian, the family means a vast network of relatives, not just parents and their children.

For this reason, family connections still affect a person's place in Syrian society. The best way to achieve success is through the help of wealthy or powerful relatives. In business and government, people prefer to hire and promote other members of their extended family. Those in a position to dispense favors will help family members before they help anyone else.

Syrians who live in rural areas tend to be more conservative in their beliefs than are educated people living in cities like Damascus and Aleppo. But obedience and loyalty to the family are important

Words to Understand in This Chapter

demographic data—statistical information about the characteristics of a population, such as the age, gender and income of the people and how these characteristics have changed over time.

hijab—a headscarf worn by Muslim women that covers their hair and neck, leaving only the face visible.

Syrian refugees, carrying their belongings, approach the border with Turkey. Syria's neighbors have fortified their borders to prevent the violence of the civil war from spilling over and destabilizing their countries.

to some extent in every social group. For example, families are often very involved in choosing marriage partners for those of the proper age. At one time—and in some rural areas—arranged marriages were common. In recent years, more young Syrians have had the freedom to choose their own spouse, but they are still expected to receive the consent of their family before marrying.

Young Syrian men and women are encouraged to marry within their extended families. Marriages between first cousins are considered ideal among Syrian Muslims, although most Christian groups forbid this practice. Syrians often find that marrying a person with close blood ties is easier than trying to divide their loyalties between two families. On the other hand, relatives sometimes view marriages between unrelated partners as a way to create useful ties with other families.

When a woman marries she takes on her husband's family ties and obligations, but her own family ties remain as well. She is always permitted to return to her parents' home. Islamic law permits a man to have more than one wife as long as he can afford it. This practice is legal, but extremely rare, in modern Syria. A

 Quick Facts: The People of Syria

Population: 17,951,639 (rank 61st in the world)
Ethnic groups: Arab 90.3%; Kurds, Armenians, and other 9.7%
Religions: Muslim 87% (official; includes Sunni 74% and Alawi, Ismaili, and Shia 13%), Christian 10% (includes Orthodox, Uniate, and Nestorian), Druze 3%, Jewish (few remaining in Damascus and Aleppo)
Language: Arabic (official), Kurdish, Armenian, Aramaic, Circassian (widely understood); French, English (somewhat understood).
Age structure:
    0–14 years: 33.1%
    15–24 years: 20.2%
    25–54 years: 37.9%
    55–64 years: 4.8%
    65 years and over: 3.9%
Population growth rate: –9.73% (rank 223rd in the world)
Birth rate: 22.76 births/1,000 population (rank 74th in the world)
Death rate: 6.51 deaths/1,000 population (rank 151st in the world)
Infant mortality rate: 15.79 deaths/ 1,000 live births (rank 103rd in the world)
Life expectancy at birth:
    total population: 68.41 years (rank 161st in the world)
    males: 61.4 years
    females: 75.84 years
Literacy: 84.1% (2011 est.)

All figures are 2014 estimates unless otherwise indicated.
Source: CIA World Factbook, 2015.

Family is very important to Syrians.

woman married to a Syrian citizen may not leave the country without her husband's permission.

Adult children usually live with their parents until they are married. Even after marriage, young couples frequently live with one set of parents for some time. Widowed parents usually live with their children and their families. People of every age are expected to obey their parents and respect their wishes.

Families often keep strict watch on the activities of unmarried women. All women are expected to behave very carefully and modestly to ensure they maintain their reputations. A damaged reputation brings dishonor to a woman's family, especially its male members. Even if she does nothing to provoke him, a man can hurt a woman's reputation simply by the way he addresses her. In rural areas women participate in agricultural work. In the cities, only about one in ten women works outside the home. Many city women who work are educated professionals.

LEISURE

Men and women rarely interact outside the home. In cities, men frequent cafes where they can talk, drink strong Turkish coffee or tea, read newspapers, play board games, and smoke cigarettes or traditional water pipes called hookahs. Women do most of their socializing at home with other women. Soccer is popular among Syrian children; they play it more commonly as a street game than as an organized sport. Basketball is another sport that has become popular in Syria.

Syrians also like to watch television and listen to the radio. Most television and radio channels available in Syria are controlled by the Syrian Arab Television and Radio Broadcasting Commission (SATRBC), a government agency. As a result, there is little freedom of the press, and most news reports have a pro-government spin. The Syrian government does not permit citizens to use satellite dishes, which would enable them to receive programming from other countries; however, it is believed that many people get around this rule in order to receive news and information that has not been censored. In 2013, the Arab news outlet Al Jazeera suspended operations in Syria, due to threats against its reporters.

According to 2009 data, roughly 4.5 million Syrians had access to the Internet. Syria is among the most restrictive countries when it comes to online content, with many sites (including Facebook and Wikipedia) banned. Bloggers or those who post challenges to the regime have been arrested and jailed. During the civil war, Syria's internet connection to the outside world has been shut off numerous times. The nonprofit organization Reporters Without Borders has named the Syrian government an "Enemy of the Internet," due to the state's restrictions on political websites and freedom of speech.

Historically, most of Syria's population lived along the coast, or around major cities like Damascus, Aleppo, Latakia, and Homs. Other populated areas include the city of Tadmur (also known as Palmyra) near the center of the country, and the area along the borders with Iraq and Turkey, particularly along the Euphrates and Khabur rivers. This map reflects population distribution prior to the outbreak of civil war in 2011; since then more than 2.25 million people have fled the country, and over 7.5 million other Syrians are internally displaced.

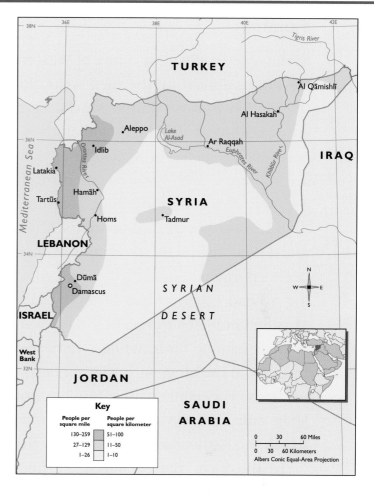

The center of Syrian social life and leisure time is the home. In the cities, many people live in modern apartment buildings. In smaller towns and villages, Syrian homes are arranged with all the rooms opening onto a central courtyard, which is usually planted with a garden and sometimes fruit trees. Homes in older sections of the cities also follow this design.

Good hospitality is an important cultural value. Syrians are eager to open their homes to guests, and mealtimes are often an important social occasion, lasting several hours. Hosting a successful get-together requires serving huge quantities of food. The entire table is often completely covered with dishes brimming with a vast array of choices. Guests are encouraged to eat as much as possible.

FASHION

Syrians generally wear a mix of Western and traditional clothing. In the cities, almost all the men wear clothes common in Europe and the United States—pants, shirts, or suits. Many women living in cities also wear Western-style clothes, but they usually dress conservatively. Loose-fitting clothing, long sleeves, and longer skirts are common, and Syrian women rarely wear pants. In rural areas, a variety of traditional ethnic costumes are often seen.

It has long been traditional for Muslim women to cover their hair and faces with veils as a sign of modesty. Although this custom declined among Syrian women during the 1970s and 1980s, wearing a head covering has become more popular in Syria and other Muslim countries in recent years. Some view it as an outward sign of their Islamic faith, while others feel less socially constrained in traditional clothing, with less concern for their safety and their reputations. Very conservative Muslim women may wear garments that leave only their eyes exposed. But most women choose to wear the **hijab**, a silk headscarf that covers the hair and neck.

In the past, the secular government has discouraged women from wearing veils and head coverings. The veil was banned on

Veiled Syrian women examine produce in a street market in Palmyra. It is typical for women to wear a head covering when in public.

Syrian college campuses in 2010, although the government lifted the ban in 2011 due to public protests.

MINORITY GROUPS

While Syria is generally considered an Arab nation, Syria is also home to a number of smaller ethnic groups that make the country more diverse. The Kurds are a minority group living in Iraq, Iran, and Turkey as well as Syria. Syrian Kurds are Sunni Muslims who speak Kurdish. Most live on the northeastern steppes where they farm and herd sheep.

Armenians are a group mainly composed of Christians who tend to settle in cities. Some belong to the Armenian Orthodox Church and others to the Armenian Catholic Church. Circassians are Sunni Muslims who originally came from southern Russia. Many are village dwellers and farmers concentrated in the Hauran and Golan areas, though a large segment of those in the Golan Heights have moved to Damascus since Israel took over the region. Assyrians live east of the Euphrates. They consist primarily of Christians who belong to the Syrian Orthodox Church, also called the Jacobite Church.

In addition to Arabic, many educated Syrians speak either French or English. Kurds speak Kurdish, which is more closely related to European languages than to Middle Eastern languages. Armenians and Circassians have their own languages. Assyrians speak Syriac, a modern version of Aramaic. Most non-Arabs in Syria speak Arabic as well as their minority language. Some of these minority languages are mainly used in religious services and ceremonies.

In the past, many nomads roamed Syria's deserts and steppes. Most of these nomads were Bedouins, a traditional group of Muslims who spoke a very old form of Arabic and pursued an independent, nomadic lifestyle. Nomads traveled all year long, setting up camp wherever they found food for their camels and sheep. They lived in tents made of camel hair and survived on a diet of milk products and occasionally some meat. Although a small number of nomads still live in the desert, today most Bedouins live in cities and villages and lead a more settled lifestyle. Bedouins are still known for their independent spirit, and many Bedouin families enjoy returning to the desert for camel races and other activities that recall their heritage.

EDUCATION

Literacy and education have been on the rise in Syria since the country gained independence. Today, education is mandatory for all children between the ages of six and eleven, although obviously schools in many areas have been disrupted by the civil war.

Primary and secondary education is free in Syria. Christians often attend their own private schools, but all schools in Syria are required to teach a curriculum provided by the state. The Syrian education system has been criticized for emphasizing memorization of facts over thinking skills. Asking questions is often discouraged in school because it is seen as a challenge to authority.

Children between the ages of six and eleven attend primary school. This is followed by three years of secondary education, much like middle school or junior high school in the United States. Three additional years of secondary education are available to a limited number of students between the ages of 15 and 18. Students have to take an exam to qualify for those spots in the secondary schools. After completing secondary schools, if students pass their exams, they may be eligible for a university education, or receive vocational or technical training. Vocational training prepares students for careers in industry, agriculture, or primary education.

More people can read and write in Syria today than ever before: almost 85 percent of the population is literate (those aged 15 or over who can read and write). But the number of literate adults in Syria is still much lower than it is in many parts of the world. Children in urban areas usually receive more years of education and attend better schools than children in rural areas, although educational opportunities for rural children have improved steadily over the last 50 years.

Syrians with university educations tend to have slightly different social values from the general population. For example, they often have more liberal attitudes about the roles of men and women in society. Educated women are far more likely to work outside the home than less-educated women.

 ## Text-Dependent Questions

1. What sport is popular among Syrian children?
2. What are the major ethnic groups living in Syria?

 ## Research Project

In recent years, as Islamist movements in many countries have stressed a return to the fundamental principals of Islam, a greater number of Muslim women have chosen to veil themselves in public. In some conservative countries, such as Afghanistan and Saudi Arabia, a woman's entire body is covered, while in secular states such as Turkey, colorful headscarves are worn but the traditional *hijab* garment is banned by the government. Using the internet, find out more about the practice of veiling, what it means to Muslim women, and how it is practiced in Syria. Write a two-page report about your findings, and share it with your class.

A view of Aleppo, Syria's largest city. The Battle of Aleppo, which began in 2012, resulted in significant casualties and the destruction of large parts of the city, due to shelling by both government and rebel forces.

Communities

With its ties to ancient civilizations, Syria is a fascinating destination for any serious student of ancient history and culture. Unfortunately, due to the violence and unrest in Syria since the civil war began, few Westerner tourists or scholars have entered the country in recent years.

Syria's coastline and mountain ranges attracted this region's early inhabitants, who established the first large settlements. Today, most Syrians live in the western half of the country, with heavy concentrations around the cities of Damascus, Aleppo, and Latakia. These cities are among the oldest in the world. About half of the country's population lives in rural areas, primarily in small village communities.

DAMASCUS

Damascus is Syria's capital and second-largest city. Many people believe it is the oldest surviving city in the world. The area of Damascus already contained settled inhabitants in 5000 BCE. It served as the capital of the province of Syria under the Roman Empire and later on, the capital of the Omayyad caliphs after the birth of Islam. Set in the foothills of the Anti-Lebanon Mountains, Damascus functioned as a "desert port" for the caravan routes of antiquity. It was the last place caravans traveling through southern Syria stopped before entering the desert, and the first place they reached upon leaving it.

Today, Damascus is a modern, growing center of government and business. The population of Damascus is growing rapidly as many people move there in search of education and opportunities not available in the country. In 2015, the city's population was estimated at about 1.4 million people.

Damascus is a place where the old and new intermingle. High-rise buildings and modern shopping districts contrast with old open-air markets known as souqs. It is the seat of a modern style of government, yet many buildings in Damascus date back to ancient times. In an effort to absorb the increasing numbers of people who have moved there in search of opportunity, the city has expanded into the nearby mountain slopes. Many of these mountain neighborhoods are overcrowded slums.

The residential **suburbs** and industrial areas that have grown up around Damascus' city center have helped cause traffic and more overcrowding. Although the older streets of Damascus tend to be

Words to Understand in This Chapter

dissident—a person who opposes official policy or the rule of an authoritarian government.
suburb—a residential district that is located near a large city, but outside of its municipal boundaries.

An aerial view of Damascus. The city in southwestern Syria is considered by many to be the oldest in the world, as Damascus was believed to have originally been settled between 8000 and 6000 BCE. Today, it is the capital of Syria.

narrow, several wide boulevards cross the center of town, with Martyrs' Square at its heart. These streets are lined with restaurants, shops, movie theaters, and hotels.

OTHER CITIES AND TOWNS

Aleppo is Syria's largest city, with a population estimated at 2.1 million. The city grew along an ancient trade route linking Mediterranean ports to the Euphrates River, and it rivals Damascus as one of the world's oldest cities. Like Damascus, it formerly served as a "desert port." It was the last large urban center on the caravan route before travelers reached the long stretch of empty steppe and desert. Before the civil war, Aleppo was a major producer of textiles. These products include silk and printed cotton fabric. Other industrial products include processed food products and leather made from the hides of animals pastured on the steppe.

Aleppo has been the location of one of the largest battles of the Syrian civil war. Rebel groups from the countryside around Aleppo began fighting government forces in February 2012, and eventually captured large areas of the city. Both sides have been criticized for their use of bombs that have caused significant damage to buildings and infrastructure. The historic Old City of Aleppo, a UNESCO World Heritage site, has been extensively damaged. In February 2015 the Syrian Army launched a new offensive, attempting to surround rebels forces in the city.

Homs is an industrial city located near the Orontes River and the Homs Gap. Its population was estimated at 650,000 in 2015, making it the third-largest city in Syria. Oil pipelines cross Homs on their way to the Homs Gap. Its location on these pipelines has made Homs an important center for oil refineries and petroleum distribution. The city has also been famous for manufacturing silk and textiles.

When Syrian protests began in 2011, Homs quickly became a stronghold for rebel groups. Syrian government forces attacked the city in May 2011, and gradually regained control of Homs. The final rebel forces withdrew in May 2014, as part of a truce agreement. However, three years of fighting have left much of the city destroyed and resulted in the deaths of thousands of civilian residents.

Hama lies north of Homs on the Orontes River. It is Syria's fifth-largest city with a population of about 315,000. One of Syria's ancient caravan towns, Hama lies at the center of a fertile agricultural region, and its people tend to be conservative. For hundreds of years, the city was home to many of the powerful families who

The excavated remains of Ugarit, an ancient city-state located on the Mediterranean coast near Latakia. The city was destroyed around 1200 BCE, and rediscovered in 1928 CE.

owned most of Syria's farmland. Today, most of Hama's citizens are Sunni Muslims. During the suppression of the Muslim Brotherhood uprising in 1982, the Syrian army destroyed large sections of the city and massacred 25,000 protesters. In 2011, the city was once again the site of anti-government protests, and the Syrian Army sent tanks into Hama as part of their crackdown on the **dissidents**, killing roughly 200 residents. Hama has remained a critical battleground in the civil war.

Hama is famous for its *norias*, huge wooden waterwheels that were once used to pump river water into pools and wells for drinking and irrigation. The smallest *norias* measure more than 30 feet (9 meters) across. Some *norias* are twice that size. *Norias* have been used to pump water in the Mediterranean region since ancient times.

Latakia, lying on the Mediterranean Sea, dates back to ancient times, and is known for its large Alawi population. Qardaha, a nearby village, is the birthplace of Hafiz al-Assad. Today, Latakia has a population of about 385,000, and is the principal port on Syria's Mediterranean coast. Almost all of Syria's imports and exports pass through Latakia. The government has put considerable investment into the city's infrastructure. The Bassel al-Assad International Airport has flights to cities within the country, as well as to neighboring Arab states. A railroad connects Latakia to the Ghab Valley along the Orontes. Facilities at the port include docks, warehouses, refrigeration buildings, and a grain silo. Merchandise for import or export is processed at a customs house near the port. Passenger boats travel between Latakia and Alexandria, Egypt; Beirut, Lebanon; Izmir, Turkey; and the island of Cyprus.

HOLIDAYS AND FESTIVALS

Syrians have quite a few government holidays when schools and businesses close. One of these is the national holiday, Evacuation Day, on April 17. Syrian Christians also celebrate Christmas and Easter. For Muslims, the most important celebrations of the year are the religious holidays of the Islamic calendar, which is based on the lunar months.

During the entire month of Ramadan, the ninth month of the Islamic calendar, Muslims are not permitted to eat or drink between sunrise and sunset. This fast, called *Sawm*, is the fourth pillar of Islam. Each evening during Ramadan families gather for a large meal after sunset, and say special prayers at this time. Muslims believe that this fasting purifies the body and strengthens the spirit.

Eid al-Fitr is a three-day celebration of the end of Ramadan. It begins on the first day of the tenth month of the Islamic calendar. It is a joyful time of celebration and thanksgiving for Allah's gifts, and fasting is forbidden. On the first morning of Eid al-Fitr, Muslims eat a large breakfast and wear their best clothing to the mosque to take part in morning prayers together. People often buy new clothes to wear for Eid al-Fitr and they get together for feasts and parties with their families and friends. Children receive gifts, money, and sweets from friends and relatives.

Many cities in Syria hold fireworks and street carnivals during Eid al-Fitr. Although the celebration lasts three days, Syrian shops and schools may close down for an entire week if the holiday falls in the middle of the week. As part of Zakat al-Fitr, a duty performed during the holiday, people also give gifts to charity.

The third pillar of Islam is the hajj, the pilgrimage to Mecca that every Muslim is supposed to undertake at least once. This pilgrimage takes place every year on the seventh to tenth days of the last month of the *Hijrah*. The rituals of the hajj include sacrificing a sheep on the final day. Many Muslims around the world participate in this custom, even when they are not in Mecca.

The celebration of the last day of the hajj is called Eid al-Adha. Those who can afford to sacrifice a sheep usually give one-third of the meat to the poor and one-third to friends and neighbors. They keep the final third for themselves and their families. This celebration is a time of feasting, prayer, and gift-giving. Schools and businesses close down for several days.

 ## Text-Dependent Questions

1. What large Syrian city is considered one of the oldest continuously inhabited places in the world?
2. Which city is the capital of Syria?
3. What two large Syrian cities are located near the Orontes River?

 ## Research Project

Two of the most important religious holidays in Islam are Eid al-Fitr, which occurs at the end of the sacred month of Ramadan, and Eid al-Adha, the last day of the *hajj* period. Choose one of these festivals, and do some research to find out more about why that particular festival is important to Muslims, how it is traditionally celebrated, and whether Syrians celebrate the festival differently than Muslims in other countries. Write a two-page report on the festival.

A battlefield on fire after shelling by government forces at Qunaitira near the Golan Heights.

Foreign Relations

For many years Syria has been considered one of the world's most insular nations, and it has often been treated as an international **pariah** due to its record of human rights violations. The Syrian government's response to protests and uprisings in 2011 drew condemnation from many nations. Today, Bashar al-Assad's administration finds itself isolated from the international community, as since 2013 some 130 foreign countries have officially recognized a coalition of rebel groups known as the National Coalition for Syrian Revolutionary and Opposition Forces as the legitimate representative of the Syrian people.

A number of foreign countries have also become involved in the civil war. Regional powers like Turkey and Saudi Arabia, where most people are Sunni Muslims, have provided financial and military support for the rebels. There have been numerous clashes on the borders with Syria's neighbors, especially Turkey, Iraq, Israel, Jordan, and Lebanon. Government leaders in the United States,

Great Britain, and France have repeatedly called for Bashar al-Assad to step aside, and has tried to negotiate a political solution to the conflict. The U.S. has also provided weapons and training to rebel groups, while imposing economic sanctions on Syria, a step taken by many European countries as well. The United Nations has sought, ineffectively, to end the violence, hosting a peace conference in 2014, and has also investigated the use of chemical weapons in Ghouta, Khan Al-Asal, and other villages during 2013. Two international organizations of Muslim states, the Arab League and the Organization of the Islamic Conference (OIC) have suspended Syria due to the civil war.

The Syrian government is not entirely without international support. Iran and Russia have provided military and financial aid, and Lebanese terrorist organization Hezbollah has sent fighters to support the Syrian Army in its conflicts with rebel groups.

SYRIA'S RELATIONS WITH ISRAEL

Since the 1940s, Syria has consistently been the most hostile and bitter of Israel's Arab neighbors. Other Arab countries have made advances in the peace process: Lebanon agreed with Israel on a permanent international boundary, and Egypt and Jordan both have diplomatic relations with the Jewish state. Syria, however, refuses to accept Israel's right to exist, and historically has encouraged and aided groups responsible for numerous terrorist attacks

 Words to Understand in This Chapter

inflexible—unwilling to change or compromise.
pariah—an outcast; a person or organization that is hated and rejected by others.

on Israeli soil. These groups include the Lebanese group Hezbollah, as well as Hamas and other militant Palestinian organizations. In the summer of 2006, when Israel invaded Lebanon in order to attack Hezbollah strongholds, Syria placed its military on alert but did not intervene directly in the conflict.

Since the 1960s, attempts to establish peace between Syria and Israel have failed on two counts. Syria refuses to make peace with Israel until all Arab countries make peace, including the Palestinian people. Syria also demands the immediate return of the entire Golan Heights up to the 1967 border as a requirement for peace. Israel has not agreed to either of these conditions. It is particularly concerned because one-third of its water supply originates in the Golan Heights. It wants guarantees from Syria that this supply will not be interrupted. The two countries also disagree on the timing of future actions. Israel wants peace and normal relations before it will with-

An Israeli Defense Force tank on patrol in the Golan Heights.

draw from the Golan Heights, and it wants to withdraw gradually, moving the border back one step at a time. Syria wants the entire Golan returned immediately and will not recognize Israel or establish relations until the withdrawal is accomplished.

There have been several clashes between Syrian and Israeli forces since the civil war began. In November 2012 three Syrian tanks entered the Golan Heights, a demilitarized zone, for the first time since Israel gained control the territory. There have also been several rocket or mortar attacks between Syrian and Israeli military forces on the border. The Syrian government has accused Israel of allowing rebel forces to cross the border in the Golan Heights and enter Israel for medical treatment.

SYRIA AND THE ARAB STATES

Historically, Syria has had a good relationship with most of the Arab states, although matters have been strained at times. Syrians have often expected other Arab states to observe their **inflexible** policy toward Israel, and relations cooled with Egypt and Jordan when those countries signed peace treaties with Israel (in 1979 and 1994, respectively). In the past, Syria's relationship with the Persian Gulf states (other than Iraq) was generally good. Many Syrians work in these wealthy oil-producing countries, and states such as Bahrain and the United Arab Emirates have given Syria considerable economic aid.

The relationship between Syria and Iraq is very complicated. Although both were ruled for many years by the Baath Party, the Syrian and Iraqi governments tended to be rivals, with each believing its version of Baath philosophy to be the correct one. Syria's support of Iran during its 1980-88 war against Iraq added to the hostility, and its participation in the U.S.-led coalition that drove Iraq out of Kuwait in the 1991 Gulf War further damaged Syrian-Iraqi relations. The two countries have frequently battled over the water rights of the Euphrates, as well as the management of the oil pipeline running from Iraq through Syria.

Despite this rivalry, Syria strongly opposed the 2003 invasion of Iraq by U.S. forces. The invasion ended Baath Party rule in Iraq, overthrowing the regime of Saddam Hussein. It also created a surge of millions of Iraqi refugees who crossed the border into Syria.

During the 2000s, as the U.S. military occupied Iraq and attempted to rebuild the state, the Syrian government was often accused of permitting terrorists to cross the Syrian border and enter Iraq, where they could sow

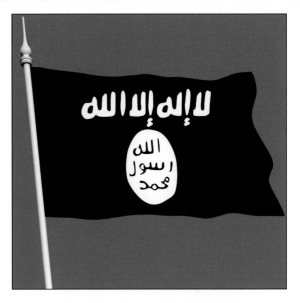

The flag of the Islamic State of Iraq and the Levant is a black banner that includes the shahada, an important Muslim statement of belief. The circle design is said to be the "seal of Muhammad," the chief prophet of Islam. Other Islamist terror organizations have adopted a black banner as well.

discord and violence. That would come back to haunt the Assad regime when the civil war began in 2011, as armed fighters from Iraq crossed the border to join anti-government rebel groups. By 2014 the Islamist organization Islamic State of Iraq and the Levant (ISIL) had seized territory in both Iraq and Syria, where it collects taxes and enforces its version of Sharia laws, including draconian punishments such as the public execution of those considered to be unfaithful to Muslim principles.

There is also a long history of tensions between Syria and its southern neighbor Lebanon. Syrian troops were stationed in the country for nearly 30 years, during which time Syria held a lot of influence over the Lebanese government. Syria has also been

Syria has long supported the Lebanese organization Hezbollah, which the United States and other countries consider a terrorist organization. These rockets were part of a 500-ton shipment of weapons to Hezbollah that was intercepted by Israeli authorities in 2009.

accused of orchestrating the assassination of Lebanese politicians, such as prime minister Rafik Hariri in 2005. Hariri's murder sparked revolts and protests in Lebanon that ultimately led Syria to withdraw its military forces later that year.

Lebanon is strategically important to Syria in its opposition to Israel. Syria has provided financial and military support for Hezbollah, a militant Shiite group operating within Lebanon that commits terrorist acts against Israel. Because the terrorists attack from Lebanese territory, Israeli retaliation tends to be against Lebanon, rather than Syria. However, the Israeli Defense Force has at times tried to cut off the Syrian support. In 2013 and 2014, for example, Israeli warplanes reportedly attacked military convoys within Syria that Israeli authorities claimed were carrying weapons meant for Hezbollah.

In addition to Hezbollah, Syria has sheltered and funded militant Palestinian groups like Hamas, which believe that Israel has no right to exist. Syria did not have close relations with Yasir Arafat's Palestinian Liberation Organization (PLO), or with the successor organization known as the Palestinian Authority, because they were willing to act independently and negotiate with Israel without consulting Syria or other Arab states about policy decisions. For many years Hamas had its headquarters in Damascus, although the group relocated in 2011 due to the civil war.

Syrian Relations with Turkey

Historically, Syria and Turkey have not had good relations. Many Syrians still resent Turkey for seizing control of the Hatay province, which historically was associated with Syria, in 1939. During the 1980s and 1990s water rights were a major issue between the two countries, as hydroelectric dams on the Euphrates River in Turkey have the potential to severely restrict the amount of river water that reaches Syria. In addition, during the 1990s the Syrian government was critical of Turkey's relationship with Israel.

In 2011, the Turkish government condemned Syria's violent response to protests and demonstrations. The Turkish government has officially stated that it would like Bashar al-Assad removed from office, and has worked actively toward that goal. Turkey has provided refuge for Syrian dissidents, and the Turkish military secretly trained military defectors who became the Free Syrian Army. This rebel group has been permitted to establish a base of operations in Turkey, and the government has provided the rebels with weapons and other military supplies.

Tensions between Syria and Turkey grew worse after Syrian forces shot down a Turkish fighter jet in June of 2012. Turkey's

Since the civil war began, Turkish president Recep Tayyip Erdogan has consistently refused to deal with the Assad regime, which he says is no longer a legitimate representative of the Syrian people.

military was ordered to deem any Syrian force that approached the border as a threat, and take action. A series of clashes between Syrian and Turkish military forces occurred in October of 2012. Turkish warplanes shot down a Syrian helicopter in 2013, and a Syrian jet in 2014.

During the early years of the war, Turkey occasionally permitted the rebel group Islamic State of Iraq and the Levant to operate within Turkey near the border with Syria. However, in 2013 ISIL operatives carried out bombing attacks in Turkey, and the Turkish military has reacted by attacking ISIL positions in Syria. Turkey has also allowed the United States—a fellow member of NATO—to use its airbases for attacks on ISIL in Syria and Iraq.

SYRIAN RELATIONS WITH IRAN

In recent decades, Iran has been Syria's closest ally. The two countries share a strong opposition to Israel, and Syria was one of the first Arab countries to recognize the Iranian state after the 1979 revolution that brought the Islamist party of Ayatollah Khomeini to power. Syria also broke with other Arab states by providing support to Iran during its 1980-88 war with Iraq. In turn, Iran has provided financial and military aid to Syria, as well as to its proxies like Hezbollah.

During the civil war, Iran has provided military and technical support to prop up the Assad regime. For example, the Iranian government has provided riot control gear and other equipment to help the Syrian government deal with public protests. It has also trained Syrian special forces to help with the crackdown on dissidents. Iranian military advisors are working with the Syrian Army.

RELATIONS WITH THE EUROPEAN UNION

In 1977, Syria signed a trade agreement with the European Union, which governed all relations between EU member states and the Syrian government. Relations were mostly friendly and based on trade of oil and financial services. However, in August 2011 the EU strongly condemned human-rights violations committed by the Assad regime in putting down anti-government protests, and banned Syria from participating in any of its financial and technical assistance programs. The EU subsequently imposed economic sanctions against the Assad government, and has prohibited Syrian citizens from traveling to Europe. The purpose of the sanctions is to encourage an end to violence and a political solution to the conflict. The EU has supported the efforts of a U.N. special envoy to negotiate a peace agreement.

By 2015, the member states of the European Union had committed more than $3.16 billion to relief efforts for Syrian refugees, both inside and outside the country. The EU also contributed funds to support international efforts to find and destroy Syrian chemical weapons and to completely dismantle the country's chemical weapons program.

One issue that concerns European leaders is the migration of Muslim citizens from their countries to Syria, where they hope to join one of the factions in the civil war. The Islamic State of Iraq and the Levant, in particular, has appealed to disaffected European Muslims, and thousands have gone to Syria despite travel bans. The issue of Europeans fighting in Syria is a matter of significant concern, both because they are contributing to the unrest but also because of fears that radicalized Muslims will attempt to return to Europe and incite religious-based strife in their home countries. By 2015, it was believed that roughly 600 Germans, 600 British, and 400 French Muslims were fighting with ISIL in Syria and Iraq, with hundreds of other fighters coming from various smaller EU states.

RELATIONS BETWEEN SYRIA AND THE UNITED STATES

Historically, the United States and Syria have had poor relations. From the U.S. perspective, Syria sponsors terrorism and denies basic civil rights to its citizens. Syria, on the other hand, is angered by U.S. support for Israel, its regional enemy.

The United States has imposed sanctions on the country since the late 1970s. It will not sell weapons to Syria, offer economic aid, or permit Syrian countries to export goods to the U.S.

Relations between the U.S. and Syria grew worse in the early 2000s. In 2002 the United States labeled Syria part of an "axis of evil," along with Iran and Iraq, other states that it believed were seeking to develop weapons of mass destruction and dominate their regional neighbors. Syria opposed the U.S. invasion of Iraq in 2003, and the U.S. cut off all diplomatic ties with Syria in 2004, claiming that Syria had become a major transit point for foreign fighters entering Iraq, as well as its interference in Lebanon and its human-rights record.

Since the civil war began, the U.S. state department has provided food, vehicles, and other non-lethal supplies to rebel groups, particularly the Free Syrian Army. At the same time, the Central Intelligence Agency (CIA) has operated a covert program to fund and arm rebel groups. Training and arming of rebel groups increased after the Assad regime was accused of using chemical weapons in 2013. The U.S. has tried to avoid providing weapons to groups with an Islamist ideology, but some supplies have fallen into their hands. In August 2014, the U.S. military began to conduct airstrikes against ISIL strongholds in both Iraq and Syria.

Officially, the U.S. government has repeatedly called for President Bashar al-Assad to step aside. The United States official-ly recognizes an organization of rebel groups called the National Coalition for Syrian Revolutionary and Opposition Forces as the legitimate representative of the Syrian people, and has been deeply involved in the United Nations' effort to work towards a negotiated political solution to the conflict.

 ## Text-Dependent Questions

1. Why has Syria historically refused to make peace with Israel?
2. What 2012 incident caused relations between Turkey and Syria to grow worse?
3. As of 2014, approximately how many French citizens had traveled to Syria to fight with ISIL?

 ## Research Project

With your school class, create a "model United Nations," assigning each student to represent a country, including Syria. Students must do some research about the country in order to properly represent its interests and understand its positions. At a meeting of the model U.N., elect a secretary-general to lead the discussion, which should be set in early 2011, before the civil war. Question the Syrian representative about the government's approach to protests, and work together to try to develop a solution that—in the opinion of your teacher—would prevent a civil war from beginning.

CHRONOLOGY

3000 BCE: Damascus and Aleppo are settled.

332 BCE: Alexander the Great invades Syria and the Middle East.

62 BCE: The Roman general Pompey invades and claims Syria for Rome.

33 CE: Christianity is founded.

330: Constantine moves the capital of the Roman Empire to Constantinople.

622: Muhammad and his followers move from Mecca to Medina; the first year of the Muslim calendar, also called the first year of the Hijrah.

635: Damascus falls to the Muslim conquerors.

636: Arab Muslims defeat the Byzantines at the Battle of Yarmouk in Syria.

7th century: The Omayyad caliphate rules from Damascus; Islam spreads across North Africa to Spain and east to western India.

8th century: The Abbasid caliphs replace the Omayyads and move the capital to Baghdad.

1055: The Turks capture Baghdad and their leader is named sultan.

1096: Christian crusaders from Europe capture Jerusalem and occupy fortresses along the Syrian coast.

1260: Mongols invade Syria and destroy much of Damascus and Aleppo.

1291 The last Crusader stronghold, at Acre, falls to the Mamluks.

1453: Ottoman Turks capture Constantinople.

1516: Ottoman Turks gain control of Syria.

1529: Sultan Suleyman the Magnificent attacks Vienna but fails to capture it.

1683: Another unsuccessful attack on Vienna leads to final defeat for the Ottomans; they are forced to sign a peace treaty.

1909: Jewish settlers in Palestine build the city of Tel Aviv.

1914: The Ottomans join World War I in alliance with the Germans.

1916: Britain and France sign the Sykes-Picot agreement, determining to divide Syria at the end of the war.

1917: The British government issues the Balfour Declaration, declaring support for a Jewish state in Palestine.

1918: British troops, assisted by Arab forces, capture Damascus from the Ottoman Turks.

1920: The French army marches on Damascus; the French occupation begins.

1928: The Nationalist Bloc forms in Syria.

CHRONOLOGY

1938: World War II begins.

1939: France gives to Turkey the province of Alexandretta, which is renamed the province of Hatay.

1940: France surrenders to Nazi Germany; Vichy France governs Syria.

1943: Syrian nationalists declare the end of the French mandate.

1945: Syria enters World War II on the side of the Allies; joins the Arab League.

1946: French troops evacuate Syria on April 17.

1947: The Baath Party officially incorporates in Syria.

1948: The State of Israel is created; the first Arab-Israeli war begins.

1949: The armistice agreement with Israel gives the land north of Lake Tiberias to Syria.

1954: Parliament and the Syrian constitution are restored after a series of military coups.

1958: Parliament, led by the majority Baath Party, votes to unite with Egypt and create the United Arab Republic, which lasts only three years.

1963: A military coup is led by a coalition of military officers, many with ties to the Baath Party.

1964: The Palestinian Liberation Organization (PLO) is organized and makes initial demands for Palestinian statehood.

1965: Syria's government assumes ownership of many businesses.

1966: Salah Jadid, a military officer and radical socialist member of Baath, takes over the government in another coup.

1967: Arab countries wage second war with Israel; Israel wins control of the Golan Heights and the Sinai Peninsula; the United Nations Security Council passes Resolution 242, which demands Israel return territories won in the war; Israel doesn't comply after failed peace negotiations with Arab countries.

1970: Jordan expels the PLO, which moves its headquarters to Lebanon; Syrian military enters Lebanon and fights alongside the PLO in civil war; Hafiz al-Assad, Jadid's Minister of Defense, seizes power in a bloodless coup.

1971: Assad becomes president of Syria in a national referendum.

1973: A Syrian constitution is drafted, giving enormous power to the president and the Baath Party; Egypt and Syria go to war with Israel.

CHRONOLOGY

1976: Civil war breaks out in Lebanon between Maronite Christians and Shiite Muslims; Syria sends troops to support the Shiites.

1979: Egypt and Israel sign a peace agreement; the Arab League withdraws Egypt's membership.

1982: Israel invades Lebanon; the Syrian military attacks the city of Hama to end the Muslim Brotherhood uprising, killing as many as 25,000 people.

1989: The Lebanese Parliament negotiates the Taif Accord, an agreement designed to restore peace and government in Lebanon; the Arab League readmits Egypt, and Syria restores relations with Egypt.

1990: Syria joins a coalition of countries fighting against Iraq in the Gulf War.

1991: Syria attends a Middle East peace conference in Madrid.

1993: Israel and the PLO sign a peace agreement in Oslo, Norway.

1996: Israel gives the Palestinian National Authority limited power and independence to rule Palestinians in the West Bank and the Gaza Strip.

2000: Syria and Israel break off peace negotiations in January; in May, Israeli troops pull out of southern Lebanon; Hafiz al-Assad dies in June, and his son Bashar takes his place.

2001: Bashar al-Assad and Yasir Arafat meet privately in March at an Arab summit to discuss terms for peace with Israel; in June, most of Syria's troops pull out of Beirut.

2002: In March, the Arab League endorses a peace initiative proposed by Crown Prince Abdullah of Saudi Arabia; Syrian troops in Lebanon move back to the Bekaa Valley in April.

2003: In January, Syria meets with Turkey and Arab nations to discuss ways to avoid involvement in expected U.S.-Iraq war; in February, the Syrian military dismantles several of its bases in northern Lebanon and moves troops out of the area.

2005: The United States withdraws its ambassador citing Syria's unwillingness to withdraw troops from Lebanon. An ambassador has yet to return.

2007: Because of the U.S.-led invasion of Iraq, thousands of refugees pour into Syria. Tougher visa restrictions are put in place in an attempt to curb the number of refugees.

2008: Syria hosts a summit on Middle East peace with France, Turkey, and Qatar. The country establishes diplomatic relations with Lebanon for the first time since the 1940s.

CHRONOLOGY

2010: In May, the United States renews sanctions against Syria, saying that it supports terrorist groups and seeks weapons of mass destruction.

2011: In March, protests begin in Damascus and Daraa, seeking the release of political prisoners. After government forces kill a number of protesters in Daraa, violent unrest spreads throughout the country. The uprising gradually turns into a civil war.

2012: The United Nations Security Council condemns the Syrian government's use of heavy weaponry against rebel forces, as well as the killing of civilians. In June, the Free Syrian Army captures much of Aleppo. In November, the leaders of several major opposition forces meet in Qatar, and agree to form the National Coalition for Syrian Revolutionary and Opposition Forces. The United States, as well as other countries, recognize the National Coalition as the legitimate representative of the Syrian people. Islamist groups fighting in Syria refuse to join the National Coalition, however.

2013: The insurgency in Syria intensifies. Islamist groups fighting in Iraq and Syria form the Islamic State of Iraq and the Levant (ISIL), which is able to capture and hold territory in both countries. The Assad government is suspected of using chemical weapons in the conflict.

2014: The United Nations holds peace talks in January and February, but Assad refuses to relinquish power to a transitional government and the talks fail. In June, the Islamic State of Iraq and the Levant declares a caliphate in the territory they control, stretching from Aleppo in northwestern Syria to the eastern Iraqi province of Diyala. They rename their group Islamic State (IS), although most Western observers continue to refer to the group as ISIL.

2015: In January, Kurdish forces drive ISIL guerrillas out of Kobane, on the Syria-Turkey border. A U.S.-led military coalition continues to launch airstrikes against ISIL in both Iraq and Syria.

autonomy—the right of self-government.

BCE and CE—an alternative to the traditional Western designation of calendar eras, which used the birth of Jesus as a dividing line. BCE stands for "Before the Common Era," and is equivalent to BC ("Before Christ"). Dates labeled CE, or "Common Era," are equivalent to Anno Domini (AD, or "the Year of Our Lord").

caliphate—an Islamic theocratic state, in which the ruler, or caliph, has authority over both the spiritual and temporal lives of his subjects and all people must obey Islamic laws.

civil society—the sum total of institutions, organizations, and groups promoting social and civic causes in a country (for example, human rights groups, labor unions, arts foundations) that are not funded or controlled by the government or business interests.

colonialism—control or domination by one country over an area or people outside its boundaries; the policy of colonizing foreign lands.

ideology—a system of beliefs, values, and ideas forming the basis of a social, economic, or political philosophy.

Islamist—a Muslim who advocates the reformation of society and government in accordance with Islamic laws and principles.

jihadism—adherence to the idea that Muslims should carry out a war against un-Islamic groups and ideas, especially Westerners and Western liberal culture.

nationalism—the belief that shared ethnicity, language, and history should form the basis for political organization; the desire of people with a common culture to have their own state.

Pan-Arabism—a movement seeking to unite all Arab peoples into a single state.

self-determination—determination by a people of their own future political status.

Sharia—Islamic law, based on the Qur'an and other Islamic writings and traditions. The Sharia sets forth the moral goals of an Islamic society, and governs a Muslim's religious political, social, and private life.

Shia—the smaller of Islam's two major branches, whose rift with the larger Sunni branch originated in seventh-century disputes over who should succeed the prophet Muhammad as leader of the Muslim community.

Sunni—a Muslim who belongs to the largest branch of Islam.

Wahhabism—a highly conservative form of Sunni Islam practiced in Saudi Arabia.

Zionism—the movement to establish a Jewish state in Palestine; support for the State of Israel.

FURTHER READING

Ball, Warwick. Syria: *A Historical and Architectural Guide.* Northampton: Interlink, 2006.

Danahar, Paul. *The New Middle East: The World After the Arab Spring.* New York: Bloomsbury Press, 2013.

Davis, Scott C. *The Road from Damascus: A Journey Through Syria.* Seattle, Wash.: Cune Press, 2003.

Erlich, Reese. *Inside Syria: The Backstory of Their Civil War and What the World Can Expect.* New York: Prometheus Books, 2014.

Hokayem, Emile. *Syria's Uprising and the Fracturing of the Levant.* London: International Institute for Strategic Studies, 2014.

Joffe, George. *A Century of Arab Revolution: The Legacy of Empires.* London: I.B. Tauris, 2015.

Mansfield, Peter. *A History of the Middle East.* 4th ed. revised and updated by Nicholas Pelham. New York: Penguin Books, 2013.

Rubin, Barry. *The Truth about Syria.* New York: Palgrave Macmillan, 2008.

Schwedler, Jillian. *Understanding the Contemporary Middle East.* Boulder, Colo.: Lynne Rienner Publishers, 2013.

Sekulow, Jay. *Rise of ISIS: A Threat We Can't Ignore.* New York: Howard Books, 2014.

Stern, Jessica, and J.M. Berger. *ISIS: The State of Terror.* New York: Ecco, 2015.

Wien, Peter. *Arab Nationalism: The Politics of History and Culture in the Modern Middle East.* New York: Routledge, 2015.

Zisser, Eyal. *Commanding Syria: Bashar al-Asad and the First Years in Power.* London: I.B. Tauris, 2006.

www.state.gov/r/pa/ei/bgn/3580.htm

The U.S. State Department website has a thorough section on the background of Syria, including its economics, politics, and other information.

https://www.cia.gov/library/publications/the-world-factbook/geos/sy.html

The CIA World Factbook website provides a great deal of statistical information about Syria and its people. It is regularly updated.

www.mideasti.org

An extensive resource geared to educate Americans about the Middle East. This academic site includes loads of information for research.

www.un.org/english

The English-language web page for the United Nations can be searched for Syria-related stories and information.

www.bbc.com/news

The official website of BBC News provides articles and videos on important international news and events related to the Middle East and elsewhere.

www.aljazeera.com

The English-language website of the Arabic news service Al Jazeera provides articles and videos on breaking news, as well as feature stories that provide background material, including profiles of leaders and essays reacting to major events.

www.fpri.org

The website of the Foreign Policy Research Institute includes informative essays by FPRI scholars on events in the Middle East.

INDEX

Numbers in **bold italic** refer to captions.

INDEX

PICTURE CREDITS

Senior Consultant **CAMILLE PECASTAING, PH.D.**, is acting director of the Middle East Studies Program at the Paul H. Nitze School of Advanced International Studies at Johns Hopkins University. A student of behavioral sciences and historical sociology, Dr. Pecastaing's research focuses on the cognitive and emotive foundations of xenophobic political cultures and ethnoreligious violence, using the Muslim world and its European and Asian peripheries as a case study. He has written on political Islam, Islamist terrorism, social change, and globalization. Pecastaing's essays have appeared in many journals, including *World Affairs* and *Policy Review*. He is the author of *Jihad in the Arabian Sea* (Hoover Institution Press, 2011).

The **FOREIGN POLICY RESEARCH INSTITUTE (FPRI)** provided editorial guidance for this series. FPRI is one of the nation's oldest "think tanks." The Institute's Middle East Program focuses on Gulf security, monitors the Arab-Israeli peace process, and sponsors an annual conference for teachers on the Middle East, plus periodic briefings on key developments in the region.

Among FPRI's trustees are a former Undersecretary of Defense, a former Secretary of the Navy, a former Assistant Secretary of State, a foundation president, and numerous active or retired corporate CEOs, lawyers, and civic leaders. Scholars affiliated with FPRI include a Pulitzer Prize–winning historian; a former president of Swarthmore College; a Bancroft Prize–winning historian; and a former Ambassador and senior staff member of the National Security Council. And FPRI counts among its extended network of scholars—especially its Inter-University Study Groups—representatives of many diverse disciplines, including political science, history, economics, law, management, religion, sociology, and psychology.

ANNE MARIE SULLIVAN received her Bachelor of Arts degree from Temple University and has worked in the publishing industry as a writer and editor. She lives in suburban Philadelphia with her husband and three children. This is her second book for school students.